Conscious Love

Previous Books by Richard Smoley

Forbidden Faith: The Secret History of Gnosticism

The Essential Nostradamus

Inner Christianity: A Guide to the Esoteric Tradition

Hidden Wisdom: A Guide to the Western Inner Traditions
          (with Jay Kinney)

First Flowering: The Best of the Harvard Advocate, *1876–1976* (editor)

Conscious Love

Insights from Mystical Christianity

Richard Smoley

JOSSEY-BASS
A Wiley Imprint
www.josseybass.com

Published by Jossey-Bass
A Wiley Imprint
989 Market Street, San Francisco, CA 94103   www.josseybass.com

Jossey-Bass books and products are available through most bookstores. To contact Jossey-Bass directly call our Customer Care Department within the United States at 800-956-7739, outside the United States at 317-572-3986, or via fax at 317-572-4002.

Jossey-Bass also publishes its books in a variety of electronic formats. Some content that appears in print may not be available in electronic books.

Excerpts from *Love's Alchemy: Poems from the Sufi Tradition* by David and Sabrineh Fideler reprinted with permission of New World Library, Novato, California; www.newworldlibrary.com.

Biblical quotations are from the Authorized King James Version unless otherwise noted.

Library of Congress Cataloging-in-Publication Data
Smoley, Richard, date.
    Conscious love : insights from mystical Christianity / Richard Smoley.
—1st ed.
        p. cm.
    Includes bibliographical references and index.
    ISBN 978-0-7879-8870-8 (cloth)
1. Love—Religious aspects—Christianity. 2.   Mysticism.   I. Title.
BV4639.S637 2008
241'.4—dc22

                                                        2007044999

Printed in the United States of America
FIRST EDITION
HB Printing   10 9 8 7 6 5 4 3 2 1

Contents

For Nicole

Acknowledgments

To those in my life who have taught me what love is, immeasurable thanks are due. To those in my life who have taught me what love is *not*, thanks are equally due, if more equivocally felt.

In the specific context of this book, I would first of all like to thank my agent, Giles Anderson, for his guidance and support through all stages of this process, as well as Sheryl Fullerton and Julianna Gustafson, my editors at Jossey-Bass. I'm deeply grateful to them for understanding what I wanted to accomplish and helping me realize it in the most effective way possible. I'd also like to thank Carol Hartland and Alison Knowles for their invaluable help in the production process and Bruce Emmer for his deft and insightful work in copyediting.

I would also like to thank my friend Ptolemy Tompkins, who as I was writing this had the uncanny knack of sending me just the right book that would help me amplify my thoughts and when it was written provided me with excellent advice about the finished product. Thanks are also due to Vlad Shilinis, who made some excellent points about the limitations of American cultural perspectives.

Finally, I would like to express my gratitude to David and Sabineh Fideler for permitting me to quote verses from their superb collection *Love's Alchemy: Poems from the Sufi Tradition* and to the Foundation for Inner Peace of Mill Valley, California, for permission to quote from *The Song of Prayer*.

R.S.

Be competent money-changers!

—Jesus Christ

Introduction

No subject in human life shows up one's limitations quite as much as love. Its universality exposes the limits of one's vision, even of one's soul. The monk grasps love from his perspective, the romantic from another; even whores and libertines have their insights. But the very fervor with which they clutch at their own little corners of this immeasurable continent suggests that they may not be able to raise their eyes and see the whole vista.

These reflections hold doubly true for anyone who sets out to write on this subject. If he sings the praises of a bloodless "spiritual" love, he will be suspected—with good reason—of adoring an abstraction while fearing or loathing the actuality. If he characterizes love as nothing more than the workings of genes and hormones, he lays himself open—with equally good reason—to the charge of reductionism, of simplistically equating the deepest longings of the human soul with mindless chemical processes. The clinician's blinders are as thick as the romantic's.

Such are my reservations as I start to write this book. They also arise out of my disappointments with the previous literature, vast as it is, on love. But then all books spring from dissatisfaction. If an author felt that the existing works covered the subject adequately, he would have no reason to write another.

Still, it often seems to me that the conventional wisdom about love is wrong or at least grossly simplistic. With romantic love, for example, for at least a generation it has been standard doctrine that only mature, committed relationships constitute love in the true sense. The theory runs something like this: In the beginning there is infatuation. A person projects her (or his) inner longings onto another, but this is little more than self-delusion. Eventually she will have to dissolve this childish passion, see her beloved as he truly is, and do the hard and painful work of constructing a real relationship.

We don't need much historical insight to see the shadow of the old Puritans in this supposedly modern portrait. True love is mature; it requires hard work; its joys are offset by its duties and obligations. By the same token, immature feelings cannot be love, not in the true sense; such things are not to be taken seriously. But who handed down this verdict? Not long ago I was talking with an old friend of mine who has been married, more or less happily, to the same woman for twenty years. For some reason I asked him who was the woman he loved most in his life. He answered in a shot: it was a girl he had a crush on in the eighth grade. He never had a relationship with this girl, had probably never gone out with her, but that was his reply. I might have given a similar answer myself. Someone may say this is puppy love and would not have stood the test of time. Granted—but who says that love has to be mature or that it has to last forever? The novelist Robert Musil once observed that the duration of a friendship imposes as many obligations as its intensity. In the same spirit, one might say that the intensity of a love endows it with as much legitimacy as its duration. Most of the time love does *not* last forever. It comes and goes by its own mysterious logic; like the spirit, it bloweth where it listeth. Even if there is reason for extolling mature, committed relationships, why then are we obliged to deny the name of love to everything else or to grant it some secondary status?

I will deal with romantic love more fully in Chapter Two, but for now let me simply say that our definitions of love in any sphere are often muddled. We want it to be other than it is, we arbitrarily pick out one form and hold it up as the true kind or the only kind, or our exposure to what the world calls love is so distorted as to blind us to the reality. A child is beaten every day by her parents, who all the while howl about how much they love her. What will she think when she grows up? All she knows is that love is a dreadful thing and is to be avoided at all costs. At the same time, under the surface she realizes instinctively—as we all do—that love is naturally desirable. But her experience can only lead her to warped conclusions. She may seek it and fail to find it, or she may seek out something harmful and imagine it is love, or she will find love and run away from it without knowing why. Probably there are few of us who are entirely free of such confusions. They are not matters of mere semantics. They're embedded in the recesses of our minds, and the restlessness and unhappiness that we see so often in ourselves is evidence of their handiwork.

What, then, is love? One of my favorite definitions is Charles Bukowski's. He defines it as "the common sense to care very much for something very good."[1] If I were to offer my own, I would say that love is what unites *self* and *other*. This is as simple and naked a characterization as I can conceive. It does not say what this union is or should be, whom or what it should include or exclude, or how long it should last. And yet even at this stage we can see that love's dynamic reflects what may be the greatest mystery in the universe—what exactly is *self* and what is *other*.

On the face of it, the answer seems obvious. The self is defined by the limits of the body: whatever goes on within this perimeter is *self*. What is *other* is whatever lies outside these boundaries. And yet the issue is not so simple. Take self-love. Who is the lover here, and who is loved? The same person. But is this really the case? Or is it rather that this so-called self-love is really a love felt by one part of the self for another part? Which, then, is the real self? Which is the *other*? Does this other feel love in turn?

The question is no easier when it involves more than one person. One of the most common motifs in love poetry is the idea that the other is, or becomes, the same as oneself. In his poem "The Ecstasy" John Donne writes:

> But as all several souls contain
> Mixture of things, they know not what,
> Love, these mixed souls doth mix again,
> And makes both one, each this and that.

Cicero says much the same thing about friendship, observing that in it man "seeks another with whom he can mingle his soul so as practically to make one out of two."[2]

Such ecstatic union is not limited to humans. The French biologist Jean Rostand describes the conjugal habits of a certain type of paramecium. For the most part, the creatures of these species reproduce like any single-celled organism: they split in two through the process called mitosis. Every now and then, however, they begin to act peculiarly. They swim about in agitation, colliding and striking at each other with their cilia. Then each paramecium unites with another until all are joined. Rostand observes:

> The two *paramecia* that have joined—*conjugated*—now press close together, mouth to mouth. This coming together, this embrace, is followed by a still more intimate contact: the members enclosing their respective protoplasms blur, then fade at the forepart of the body, so that the two conjugant cells are now, so it seems, *open to each other, in each other.*

Over the next fifteen hours the pair will join their nuclei together to form a "mixed nucleus, a nucleus of conjugation." When this process is complete, the two paramecia separate again. As Rostand says, "Nothing, in appearance, distinguishes the infusorium from what it was before the marriage. And yet it has become essentially different; it has expelled an important part of its nuclear substance . . . , and above all, having received from its partner exactly as much as it has given, it has become *half the other*."[3]

In this curious biological phenomenon, we see in miniature the tension that contorts the entire universe. A thing, a self, an "I" wants to assert its existence, wants to stake out its territory in the face of everything else that exists. And yet this pure solitude is unendurable. This self also feels an overwhelming urge to go past the membrane it has formed—it is driven to transcend and possibly shatter its own limits. The paramecium blends its protoplasm with another's; the lover seeks to merge with the beloved. It's not hard to see why love and death are so frequently paired. It's tempting to go one step further and find the source of the great mystery of creation and destruction here in this dynamic. As early as the fifth century B.C., the Greek philosopher Empedocles said that love and strife are the two forces that form the universe.

Nevertheless, if we look at other cultures and civilizations, we will find that love does not necessarily occupy center stage. A friend of mine recently made it a kind of spiritual discipline to read the Qur'an in full, a task she found irksome not because of its difficulty but because of the irritation it caused her. Once she cried out in exasperation, "The Qur'an says almost nothing about love!"

Nor does Buddhism. Mahayana Buddhism (which is merely one line of the tradition) speaks chiefly of compassion. While there are Buddhist practices that cultivate *metta* (loving-kindness), the idea of compassion is never far away. And compassion is a different thing from love: compassion inevitably evokes the notion of suffering; and indeed the first of the Buddha's Four Noble Truths is that life is suffering. You can really have compassion only for those who suffer (although, according to Buddhism, this category includes all sentient beings), but you can love regardless of whether or not you sense any suffering in your beloved. Indeed, certain Buddhist practices deliberately cultivate compassion as an antidote to what "may turn into an inordinate clinging to the love-object," as Herbert V. Guenther, a scholar of Tibetan Buddhism, points out.[4]

One could say similar things about most, if not all, the other great world faiths. For them, love is of value, even of high value, but not necessarily of supreme value. Consequently, at its core, the problem of love seems to be a problem of Christianity. It's easy to overlook this fact. We tend to forget that although love has existed as long as the human race itself, it was Christ who posited this mysterious force as being at the center of experience. The Law of Moses told the Jews to "love the Lord thy God with all thy heart and all thy soul and all thy mind" and to "love thy neighbor as thyself," but it was Christ who chose these as the two great commandments.

I am not saying that this emphasis on love makes Christianity superior to other religions. It's rather that we in the West extol love because we consciously or unconsciously remain Christians, no matter what box we may check under "religion" on the census form. If we're constantly told that "love is the answer" and "all you need is love," it's largely due to the pervasiveness of Christianity. Are these claims true? Does love really deserve to stand on the pinnacle of veneration? Since it is Christianity that makes these claims, it is to Christianity that we will have to turn in order to see if love really is, as Dante writes, both the force "that moves the sun and the other stars" and the force "by which the world is turned to chaos."[5]

The perspective from which I'll be examining these issues may seem an unusual one and will at times cut against many Christians' notions of received truth, so it calls for some explanation at the start. I will be basing my insights on *mystical* or *esoteric Christianity*. (Although these terms are not exactly equivalent, I will be treating them as such in this book.)[6] Often the word *esoteric* conveys the sense of something abstruse and far removed from us. Etymologically, however, it means the exact opposite. It's derived from Greek roots meaning "further in." Esotericism takes us further into ourselves to discover certain truths that are hidden from the surface of materiality.

Esotericism is not a new religion or some alternative sect of a conventional religion. Rather it is the essential truth that lies at the core of all religions, although they may express this truth differently and, it may seem, contradictorily. Stating (or restating) this doctrine in Christian terms was in fact the purpose of my earlier book *Inner Christianity*. While the differences between religions are not to be minimized (if only because religion itself has made a business of maximizing them), these differences are to be seen in the light of central truths that are universal precisely because they are true. That's why in this book I've cited texts from other traditions, which sometimes express some of these ideas more clearly than the writings of Christianity proper.

According to esoteric teaching, many of the ideas expressed in Christianity are not and were never meant to be taken as literal truths but refer to states of consciousness "further in" ourselves. Even the story of Christ is not to be taken at face value; rather it symbolizes our own predicament and destiny as humans. The God-man is born on earth; he lives and works and plays his part on the stage of history. He is crucified in wretchedness and humiliation on a cross known as time and space. Ultimately, however, it does not matter. He is resurrected in a higher, purer form because what is truly real in him can never die; it can only be transformed.

This is the story of Christ. It is our story as well. Intuitively we know it to be so, and it is this fact, rather than the endless proselytizing and self-aggrandizement of the faith's innumerable sects and denominations, that I believe most truly accounts for the enormous success of Christianity around the world. If we have some more conscious glimpse of this truth—and probably we will never have more than glimpses—we will not only know ourselves better but be able to love better. This is the central idea that I hope to explore in this work.

1

Kierkegaard's Error

In September 1840, the budding philosopher Søren Kierkegaard realized he had made a terrible mistake. It was one of the sort many men make. Some manage to correct it in time; some do not. It had to do with a proposal of marriage, and in this case at least, it led to an extraordinarily romantic tale.

The great lovers of history and literature are usually characters with dash, and their stories are highly dramatic, laced with glamour, intrigue, and sometimes violence. But Kierkegaard was a rather unromantic figure. The surviving pictures of him are sketches, chiefly caricatures (he did not have his portrait painted or his daguerreotype taken), but they show him as a small, stoop-shouldered man with side whiskers and eyeglasses, which no doubt detracted from the effect of the dapper attire he was fond of wearing. His romance took place in the parlors of the Copenhagen bourgeoisie. Despite this staid backdrop, Kierkegaard's romance has the aura of one of the great love stories of Western history.

His beloved was a young woman named Regine Olsen. Like Kierkegaard, she belonged to the upper middle class of the Danish capital. Kierkegaard had met her in May 1837, when she was fourteen and he twenty-four. He was immediately captivated—a condition he concealed with a masterful display of wit. She, too, must have been taken by him; describing the encounter sixty years later, she remembered the strong impression he had made on her, although she could recall nothing of what he said.[1]

It was not until three years after that first meeting that Kierkegaard began to frequent the Olsen household. In September 1840, he met Regine on the street on his way to her house. No one else was at home, and she invited him in. She began to play the piano, but Kierkegaard stopped her, saying, "Oh, what do I care about music. It is you I have wanted, and have wanted these two years." Two days later he came and asked for her hand. She accepted.

Immediately afterward, Kierkegaard went into paroxysms of remorse. When Regine saw him several days later at a party, she found him "completely changed—absent and cold," as one friend recollected. Thus began several months of ambiguity and equivocation, eloquently reflected in Kierkegaard's letters to her, a series that begins with ardor and ends with curt excuses for his absence. Finally their engagement breaks off. It is she who breaks with him, but as he confesses, it is he who has provoked it. Fashionable Copenhagen denounces the young cleric as a scoundrel. Regine soon finds a new suitor, whom she marries. Kierkegaard stays single for the rest of his life.

If this were the whole story, it wouldn't be worth telling: reneging on vows of devotion is common and indeed clichéd. But it's clear that Kierkegaard didn't break with Regine because he did not love her. In a note to his brother at the end of his life, Kierkegaard directs that all his estate is to go to Regine: "To me an engagement was and is just as binding as a marriage, and that therefore my estate is her due, exactly as if I had been married to her."[2] Even if we knew nothing else about Kierkegaard, we could tell from this that he was not a cad.

Another anecdote casts more light on this unusual relationship. One day Kierkegaard rented a carriage and took Regine out for a drive to the country—something that delighted her immeasurably. But he soon turned around and took her back, "so that she could be accustomed to denying herself pleasures," according to Henrik Hertz, an acquaintance who told the story. "He should have been beaten on the a ____ for that," Hertz added.[3]

Something strange, then, was at work in Kierkegaard's feelings for Regine. In the first place, he may have fled simply because he was terrified by the prospect of his own happiness—a common reaction among melancholic types, as he was. At times his letters suggest that he is also afraid of making her miserable. Kierkegaard may give still another hint in his *Works of Love*, written in 1847: "One may make the mistake of calling love that which is really self-love: when one loudly protests that he cannot live without his beloved but will hear nothing about love's task and demand, which is that he deny himself and give up the self-love of erotic love."[4]

As grand as this sounds, it fails to explain why "love's task and demand" should automatically mean giving up "the self-love of erotic love." Regine was by far the more passionate of the two (Kierkegaard once tried to subdue her ardor by presenting her with a New Testament), so his yielding to this "self-love" might not have been totally selfish after all. But the episode with the carriage suggests that this impulse toward sacrifice runs very deep in Kierkegaard, as it does in the Christian tradition of which he is a part.

The same point was driven home to me years ago when I was a student. I was ringing in the New Year—it must have been 1978 or '79—with some friends in a seedy bar on New York's Upper East Side (seedy bars being more common there then than they are now). We found ourselves sitting next to an elderly and rather drunk Irish lady. At one point she burst out, "The Catholic Church kept me from marryin' the man I loved!"

We turned to the woman, and she launched into her story. Fifty years before in Ireland, she knew a man she was powerfully attracted to, but her religious upbringing had given her the idea that it was sinful to have these feelings. She decided that the right thing to do was marry another man, whom she did *not* desire, and she evidently lived unhappily with him ever after.

I did the only thing I could, which was to listen with the bland sympathy with which one receives confidences from a stranger at a bar, but the episode left a deep impression on me. It's curious to think that Kierkegaard, one of the finest philosophical minds of recent centuries, and an old woman who did not seem very well educated should have fallen into the same trap, but apparently they did.

The old woman lived to regret her decision; to all appearances Kierkegaard made peace with his. Both their stories raise the question of why this automatic leap into self-sacrifice and this spurning of sexuality seem so automatic in Christianity. The religion of love *par excellence*, it is also the religion of the *sublimation* of love. In its two thousand–year history, Christianity in most of its forms has unstintingly preached the superiority of spiritual love to the sexual variety. And it has just as relentlessly preached that the latter is to be sacrificed to the former.

These are not just abstract considerations. As the old woman's story suggests, this problem intrudes into relationships everywhere. From the male point of view, it can lead to the madonna-whore complex, in which the man cannot permit himself to feel sexually attracted to the woman he loves emotionally or to feel love for a woman who has sex with him. One can only wonder how many infidelities and broken marriages are due to this strange split in the Western psyche.

Where does this tension come from? Christianity owes as much, or more, to Plato than it does to Christ, and this motif of sublimation goes back to the Greek philosopher. It appears in the *Symposium*, at whose climax Socrates tells of his initiation into the mysteries of love by an old priestess named Diotima.

Diotima's instructions for finding the true meaning of love at first don't sound very Christian: "The candidate for this initiation cannot, if his efforts are to be rewarded, begin too early to devote himself to the beauties of the body." But this is only an elementary step. "Next," she continues, "he must grasp that the beauties of the body are as nothing to the beauties of the soul, so that wherever he meets with spiritual loveliness, even in the husk of an unlovely body, he will find it beautiful enough to fall in love with and to cherish." Then the devotee is to take his sights still higher and cultivate love of beauty in its more abstract forms: "The quest for the universal beauty must find him ever mounting the heavenly ladder . . . until at last he comes to know what beauty is. . . . And once you have seen it, you will never be seduced again by the charm of gold, or dress, or comely boys."[5] Love is to culminate in contemplation of the Form of Beauty, the abstract quality whose presence in earthly things is what, according to Plato, makes them beautiful.

Diotima's course in love involves increasing sophistication; the seeker passes from love of the flesh to the more abstract but finer love of the intellect. This ascent has given rise to the term *platonic love*. This picture has no real ethical component, or if it does, it is far in the background. Diotima paints the progression as an education in connoisseurship.

And yet for Kierkegaard more than two thousand years later, spiritual love is *morally* superior to physical love, and he seems to think that one of these must be sacrificed if a person is to have the other. In this he echoes much of the Christian tradition, which over the centuries grew more and more disapproving of sex in any circumstances. At first it merely urges that sex be limited to marriage. Paul advises the Corinthians to remain celibate, "even as I myself," but he also says, "Nevertheless, to avoid fornication, let every man have his own wife, and let every woman have her own husband" (1 Corinthians 7:2, 7). The *Didache* ["Teaching"] *of the Twelve Apostles*, one of the earliest Christian writings, dating probably from the early second century, simply warns, "Beware of the carnal appetites of the body."[6] The second-century allegory *The Shepherd of Hermas* (revered by many early Christians as a sacred text) urges, "Always keep your mind on your own wife and you will never go wrong. For if this desire [for another man's wife] enters your heart, you will go wrong, and if other things as evil as this enter, you will sin."[7]

This guidance is perfectly sensible. But the stance grows more rigid over the centuries to the point where the flesh is always evil and sexuality always wrong—sometimes even *within* marriage. The church father Jerome (c. 340–420) even says, " 'He who too ardently loves his wife is an adulterer.' It is disgraceful to love another man's wife at all, or one's own too much."[8] Jerome doesn't go so far as to say that sex within marriage is sinful (he would have gone against Scripture if he had), but he comes as close as he can. Like most church fathers, he regards the wedded state as a poor second choice to celibacy. Kierkegaard, eminently learned in theology, must have been influenced at least to some degree by these ideas.

Then there is the element of sacrifice. Christ's well-known command that "thou shalt love thy neighbour as thyself" (Mark 12:31) has frequently been altered by later Christianity in a subtle but crucial way. The *Epistle of Barnabas*, written probably in the first century A.D., urges, "Love your neighbour *more than* yourself."[9]

At first glance, *Barnabas* may seem to offer an improvement on Christ's original statement. After all, if it's good to love your neighbor as yourself, isn't it better to love him more than yourself? Not necessarily. Christ's original message erases distinctions; it lowers the barriers between human beings. *Barnabas*, with whatever good intentions, brings in the element of quantity, and with it a kind of cost-benefit analysis. One is presumably to calculate how much one loves another versus oneself and make sure the equation comes out right. It ultimately reinforces the barrier between self and other, thus defeating what may have been the purpose of Christ's directive.

These two threads—the antipathy to sexuality and the urge toward sacrifice—have been deeply interwoven into Christian life and thought and through them into much of Western civilization, even in today's secular society. They raise questions that underlie many perplexities of human relations. In order to experience true love, do we have to sacrifice sexuality? Still more fundamentally, does love always have to *cost* something?

Kierkegaard has no doubts on this score. In *Works of Love* he writes:

> If a lover had done something for the beloved, something humanly speaking so extraordinary, lofty, and sacrificial that we men were obliged to say, "This is the utmost one human being can do for another"—this certainly would be beautiful and good. But suppose he added, "See now I have paid my debt." Would not this be speaking unkindly, coldly, and harshly? Would it not be, if I may say it this way, an indecency which ought never to be heard, never in the good fellowship of true love? If, however, the lover did this noble and sacrificial thing and then added, "But I have one request—let me remain in debt": would this not be speaking in love?

He goes on to make a strange argument: *"Everything which shall be kept alive must be kept in its element.* But love's element is infinitude, inexhaustibility, immeasurability." Thus "to be and remain in infinite debt is in itself an expression of love's infinitude."[10] Kierkegaard no doubt intends to be both paradoxical and profound, but there's a problem with his argument. After all, what does debt involve if not the keeping of accounts? And how does one keep a reckoning of infinity? In any case, an "infinite debt" is almost certain to feel like a stifling and tiresome obligation to both parties, no matter how high-minded their aspirations.

Like the *Epistle of Barnabas*, Kierkegaard seems to be unintentionally contradicting the teaching of the Gospels. The Gospels speak constantly about debts, but inevitably the moral is the *forgiveness* of debts. The Lord's Prayer instructs us to ask God, "Forgive us our debts as we forgive our debtors" (Matthew 6:12). The Greek word *opheleimata* here literally means "debts" and not "trespasses," as it's sometimes rendered. That is, according to the teachings of Christ, Kierkegaard is wrong. It is not a question of accumulating infinite debt (which, if examined, may well uncover a subtle egotism) but rather of canceling *all* debts—one's own and others'.

This leads to the heart of our inquiry. A debt is a transaction, an exchange in which a cost is incurred. It could be argued that all conventional forms of love are transactional in this way. We discharge debts by our good deeds; we incur them when others bestow kindnesses on us. The exchanges are exact and often rigorous. Here's another view of love's "infinite debt," from Laura Kipnis's cynical but insightful *Against Love*:

> Exchanging obedience for love comes naturally—we were once children after all, whose survival depended on the caprices of love. And thus you have the template for future intimacies: if you love me, you'll do what I want or need or demand to make me feel secure and complete and I'll love you back. Thus we grow to demand obedience in our turn, we household dictators and petty tyrants of the private sphere, who are in our turn, dictated to.[11]

Debt in this sense is not a matter of sin. Nor are the demands for domestic obedience; they are not "trespasses," because most of these social transactions violate neither the law nor the dictates of morality. Favors and obligations are as much a part of the national currency as the money supply. They are not reckoned on the ledgers of the Federal Reserve, but they are calculated in our minds and hearts. These calculations lead to tremendous confusion about the nature and purpose of love.

It would be easy to launch into a tirade against the coldness of human life, in which everything is computed at a cost and nothing is free and in which personal connections are calculated by an internal system of double-entry accounting. Most of us tend to experience these limitations as an indignity, although we're usually happy to invoke them on our own behalf when necessary. My point is not to inveigh against this injustice—or rather, against this justice, since the give-and-take of human intercourse is usually rigorously exact. Instead I hope to show that there are dimensions of human existence that can transcend this level of give-and-take and can even be infused into it, enabling us to move past debt and obligation, freeing ourselves as well as others. This is what the Christian tradition means when it speaks of *agape*, sometimes defined as "unconditional love."

There are, then, two loves. One is calculated, calculating, and exact. In this book I will call it "transactional love" or "worldly love," since it underlies the operations of ordinary life. The other form is free, spontaneous, joyful, and sometimes capricious; I will call it *agape*, "unconditional love," or "conscious love." I am taking the last phrase from the spiritual teacher G. I. Gurdjieff (c. 1866–1949), who taught a version of esoteric Christianity.[12] Gurdjieff wrote:

> Love of consciousness evokes the same in response
> Love of feeling evokes the opposite
> Love of body depends only on type and polarity.[13]

These utterances may look obscure, but they make sense in light of the ideas I've sketched out. Why should conscious love "evoke the same in response"? Because it demands nothing and asks nothing. C. S. Lewis, in his celebrated book *The Four Loves*, calls it "gift-love," and this is correct, as long as we avoid confusing it with the idea of gifts given in the ordinary world, which usually have certain obligations hidden in the packaging. If the gift is genuinely free of the obligation to reciprocate (as few gifts truly are), it will evoke genuine gratitude in response. From this, love—the same kind of love—can arise.

"Love of feeling evokes the opposite." Love of feeling—emotional love in all its variants—wants to be paid in kind. The recipient senses this demand with her emotional intelligence (which is exquisitely sensitive to such Trojan horses) and sooner or later resents it. It's frequently true, of course, that the "love of feeling" is mutual. This produces complications that I will discuss in the next chapter.

"Love of body depends only on type and polarity." Gurdjieff's statement is both unassailable and fraught with mystery. Anyone who has felt the pull of a beguiling stranger at a party can attest to the power of this attraction. Even so, its workings are as hidden from us as the functioning of our mitochondria. Sacred traditions around the world have developed many different forms of the "science of types," which attempts to study this attraction. The most common version today is astrology, whose continued popularity, despite the scientists' relentless contempt, suggests that there is more to this discipline than skeptics admit. But if astrology is not totally fallacious, it's not foolproof either.

In this book I mean to show that conscious love—love that is beyond transactions—is different, qualitatively rather than quantitatively, from worldly love. It's well known that the Greek of the New Testament has four words for love (hence Lewis's title *The Four Loves*). The first is *eros*, or desire, which spans the full gamut of passionate emotions from raw lust to romantic adoration. The second is *storge*, or family love. This word comes from the Greek verb *stergein*, which has the connotation of "putting up with," which casts a rather droll light on family relations. The third is *philia*, or friendship. The fourth is *agape*.

The vocabulary of ancient Greek thus covers the gamut of human connections fairly thoroughly. English is not so well endowed. We only have one word to encompass this entire spectrum of emotions—or two, if we include the verb *like*. Because these words have to span such a wide range, they create ambiguities and confusions that lead to any amount of unhappiness.

Several years ago, walking ahead of two girls on a busy New York street, I heard a snatch of their conversation. One said to the other, "So I said to him, 'I like you but I don't love you.' So does that mean we should sleep together?" The two girls passed me on the sidewalk and I never heard the friend's reply, but I was struck by the question. It seemed to reflect a real confusion—one that was no doubt very painful to the girl—about the "debt of love": How much does one kind oblige us to feel another? How many times have we held ourselves back from saying "I love you" because we feared that it would be taken in a way we did not mean?

Agape stands apart. It has little regard for social conventions, nor, when viewed from the exterior, does it even necessarily look like love. Christ's behavior in the Gospels exemplifies *agape* in its many dimensions, but he is rarely meek and mild; often he comes across as sharp and abrupt. This Jesus has little to do with the Good Shepherd of sentimental art.

This contrast between *agape* and worldly love helps us peer into love's most elusive mystery: Why should we love at all? Because it feels good? But it doesn't always feel good. Because the social contract demands it? But what happens when society isn't looking? Because God is looking, then? In that case, we are loving only to buy favors from God. The twentieth-century Russian philosopher Nicolas Berdyaev sums the problem up well when he says that in Christianity,

> love for men, for neighbors, friends and brothers in spirit, is either denied or interpreted as an ascetic or philanthropic exercise useful for the salvation of one's soul. Personal love for man and for any creature is regarded as positively dangerous for salvation and as leading one away from the love of God. One must harden one's heart against the creature and love God alone. This is why Christians have often been so hard, so cold hearted and unfeeling in the name of virtues

useful for their salvation. Love in Christianity became rhetorical, conventional and hypocritical. There was no human warmth in it.[14]

In speaking of this kind of love as an "exercise useful for the salvation of one's soul," Berdyaev reminds us that transactionality is not so easy to avoid. Even when it inspires acts that are apparently selfless, the motive of buying favor with God (or avoiding punishment from him) may be hiding under the surface. The love of would-be saints often has a whiff of hypocrisy; they seem to be obeying Christ's injunction to lay up treasures in heaven as if they were making deposits in a bank. Berdyaev adds, "Ordinary sympathy and compassion is more gracious and more like love than this theological virtue."[15] An earlier Russian philosopher of love, Vladimir Solovyov, expresses the same sentiment: "This unfortunate spiritual love reminds one of the little angels in old paintings, which have only a head, then wings and nothing more."[16]

Yet "ordinary sympathy and compassion" do exist. When they are present, they seem like the most natural things in the world. Sociobiologists sometimes contend that this altruism is nothing more than the work of selfish genes making sure that other genes like themselves will survive (a subject I'll discuss in Chapter Four). So it may be, at a certain level. Unfortunately, the present age has been far too accepting of reductionistic answers that drain the blood from our spiritual and emotional lives. If our civilization slits its own throat, the weapon it uses may turn out to be Occam's razor.

We don't have to reject the insights of the hard sciences in order to go beyond them. Human life, seen from an ordinary perspective, is proverbially mysterious, so we may feel justified in trying to view it from higher and deeper dimensions. This takes us into the realms of the mystical and the esoteric. While I will go further into these ideas in later chapters, let me at least say here that one of the crucial steps in the journey is to pass through what Christ calls the "strait gate" (Matthew 7:13). At this level of awakening, the individual self is surpassed, and one realizes that paradoxically, what is most deeply and intimately "I" is precisely the dimension of being that we share with others. The primordial tension between "self" and "other" is thus transcended or simply melts away into a higher Self. This Self is impersonal: it does not belong to us; we belong to it. Plotinus, a Greek philosopher of the third century A.D., alluded to this truth in his dying words: "Strive to bring back the god in yourselves to the God in the All."[17] Ultimately, the "I" is a "we."

To pass through this "strait gate" fully and consciously is sometimes called *liberation*. It's easy to see why. To realize that one's inmost, truest "I" is universal and thus indestructible in itself sweeps away many of our preoccupations with personal survival, whatever form these may take. This is the truth that sets us free.

At this point love arrives into a totally new dimension. As long as we see ourselves as isolated identities bartering and swapping and squabbling for survival, love will remain trapped on the level of the transactional. But if consciousness awakens to the point where it can identify with the universal mind, it can relax its grasp. It begins to view things from a broader perspective, and what is perhaps most important, it can see the ego from a remove, as one of many egos operating in the world, none of them particularly privileged. At this point one becomes far more capable of kindness and giving that are free of ulterior motives. This perspective is what I identify with conscious love.

The conditions for this awakening are varied and almost limitless. Some people may have a powerful but unbidden experience of the sacred that opens up their awareness suddenly and immediately. (William James, in his classic work *The Varieties of Religious Experience*, categorized these as "conversion experiences.") Others have a glimpse of awakening that then requires many years to develop and integrate. Still others find that they achieve nothing except by dint of many years of deliberate inner work. In the vast majority of cases the process is a long one—usually a matter not of years but of decades.

What I am saying here may seem to imply that conscious love is the prerogative of a spiritual elite. This is not really true. While only a few may have a clear sense of the whole range of steps in this process, the fundamental truth of this higher love underlies much of even everyday behavior. It is probably why Berdyaev's "ordinary sympathy and compassion," without which life would be unendurable, are so common and so natural (as they are, despite our constant complaints to the contrary). It encourages and justifies forgiveness, that mysterious salve that heals so many wounds: "One forgives to the extent that one loves," observed La Rochefoucauld.[18] It may also explain why simple, kind-hearted people often display a goodness that outshines the pretensions of would-be saints.

At the same time, we seem to need more than ordinary goodness and kindness. There is something in the human enterprise that is concerned with increasing consciousness. We not only want to experience something, we also want to know why it is the way it is—and what is still more crucial, we have an unstinting urge to experience it in full awareness, like Odysseus, who had himself lashed to the mast of his ship so he could hear the song of the Sirens. Hence the journey to conscious love could be seen as central to human experience.

If I were to stop here, I would be in full agreement with the mainstream Christian tradition, which almost unanimously proclaims the superiority of *agape* to love in its coarser varieties. And yet like most truths, this is only a partial truth. To see why, it's useful to turn to the meaning of the Greek word *agape*. Liddell and Scott's Greek lexicon makes an often overlooked point about the nuances of this word, noting that *agape* can imply "regard rather than affection."[19] And indeed the usage of this word in the Greek of all periods generally suggests something slightly remote and disinterested. This suggests that the purity of conscious love, taken by itself, can be rather cold and bloodless. Divorced from the more ambiguous but more engaged "love of the world," *agape* turns into the arid theological virtue that Berdyaev deplores.

Many wedding ceremonies include a reading of Paul's famous encomium to love from 1 Corinthians: "Love is patient and kind; love is never boastful," and so on (1 Corinthians 13:1–13). This passage is almost never read in the King James Version because the King James translates the Greek *agape* here not as "love" but as "charity." And yet "charity," with its impersonal, disinterested flavor, is probably closer to the meaning of Paul's Greek than is "love," leading one to ask, exactly what sort of love are couples pledging to each other when they get married? Are they being implicitly told to confound one kind of love with another, like the girl I overheard on the street?

It's hard to see how conscious love, even in its highest reaches, will totally eradicate our urges for human closeness and companionship and sexuality (however much the saints of the world, real and supposed, seem to suggest that this is desirable). There are said to be holy people who have reached such pinnacles of achievement. I have never met any. Ultimately, we are joined to one another by our needs and transactions as much as by anything else, and no degree of sanctity is likely to change this fact. For most of us, probably even the best of us, love comprises an intense, even violent dynamic between an impartial sublimity—the sense "that I was blessèd and could bless,"[20] as W. B. Yeats put it—and the sizable part of our nature that keeps a watchful eye out for its own interests. It is our very humanity that spans this whole range of feeling, and if we despise and revile one section of it, we risk making ourselves not more but less human.

Conscious love is not, or is not entirely, freedom from drives or passions or self-interest but rather freedom *within* them. It is capable of taking ordinary human relations as they are, in their full nakedness, while at the same time softening and mitigating their harsher aspects. In this process, the world as we experience it becomes less severe and hard-edged, and reality itself starts to seem more accommodating and malleable.

To see how this can operate in practice, I'll discuss each of the common forms of love—and their relationship to conscious love—in turn. When I set out to write this book, I intended to follow the familiar schema of the four loves, but as I became immersed in writing, that approach did not help me organize my thoughts. I found it more natural to break down the discussion into romantic love, marriage, family love, friendship, and *agape* or conscious love. Even these, however, did not quite fill the bill. It also seemed necessary to discuss love in a more universal sense—compassion and concern for humanity as a whole, particularly as manifested in the drive toward social justice and the role each individual is called to play in this effort. These divisions are perhaps arbitrary, but it would be no less so to organize the discussion around the nuances of Greek terms: language itself, after all, only corresponds in a rough and untidy way to reality.

2

Beyond the Equation

The life of a pickup artist is a peculiar one—or so it would seem from Neil Strauss's bizarre but fascinating book *The Game: Penetrating the Secret Society of Pickup Artists*. For the adepts of this arcane practice, meeting women is a matter not of luck but of skill. The artist has to find his mark, attract her attention, and demonstrate his value—all in a few short minutes. He then has to "disarm the obstacles," "isolate the target," and "create an emotional connection," to be followed by a physical one. Sex is not necessarily the object of a first meeting, but a successful artist will finish his initial encounter at least with a "kiss-close."

This strange term is a borrowing from the jargon of salesmen, who refer to a sale as a "close." It's only one example of the subculture's argot: *sarger* (pickup artist), *target* ("the woman in a group whom the pickup artist desires"), *IOI* (indication of interest), *hook point* ("the moment in a pickup when a woman . . . decides that she enjoys the company of a man who has recently approached her and doesn't want him to leave"), and *ASD* ("anti-slut defense: the maneuvers some women make to avoid taking responsibility for initiating or agreeing to sex; or in order to avoid appearing slutty to the man she is with, to her friends, to society, or to herself").[1]

The techniques are not necessarily sophisticated. There is *peacocking*—wearing a flashy piece of clothing or jewelry to distinguish yourself from the AFCs (average frustrated chumps); attracting a woman's attention with some minor feat of magic or mind reading (ask a woman to think of a number from one to ten; almost always it will be seven, we're told); even handwriting analysis. The tricks are so transparent that one could doubt whether a woman of even the dimmest intelligence would fall for them. Strauss answers:

> I'd heard . . . intelligent women say, "That wouldn't work on me." . . . Yet minutes or hours later, I'd see them exchanging phone numbers—or saliva—with one of the boys. The smarter a girl is, the better it works. Party girls with attention deficit disorder generally don't stick around to hear the routines. A more perceptive, worldly, or educated girl will listen and think, and soon find herself ensnared.[2]

Of all the sarger's techniques, one of the most intriguing is the *neg* (short for "negative"): "an ambiguous statement or seemingly accidental insult delivered to a beautiful woman a pickup artist has just met, with the intent of actively demonstrating to her (or her friends) a lack of interest in her." Negs can range from the comparatively subtle ("I like that skirt. Those are real popular these days") to the ham-handed (Strauss recommends keeping a blacklight on hand "for pointing out lint and dandruff on girls' clothing").[3]

One man who might have approved of this tactic is Socrates. In Plato's dialogue the *Lysis*, Socrates converses with two young men, one of whom, Hippothales, is, in true ancient Greek fashion, enamored of the other, Lysis. Socrates warns Hippothales, "All connoisseurs . . . in matters of love are careful of praising their favorites before they have won them, from their doubts as to the result of the affair. Moreover, your beauties, when lauded and made much of, become gorged with pride and arrogance." Later, when Lysis challenges him on some points, Socrates says in an aside, "On receiving this reply from Lysis, I turned my eyes on Hippothales, and was on the point of making a great blunder. For it came into my head to say, This is the way, Hippothales, that you should talk to your favorite, humbling and checking instead of puffing him up and pampering him, as you now do."[4]

Women know the same secret. A feminine equivalent of Strauss's bible of seduction is a best seller from the mid-1990s called *The Rules: Time-Tested Secrets for Capturing the Heart of Mr. Right,* by Ellen Fein and Sherrie Schneider. On the surface, there might seem to be nothing further from the sarger's ostentation than the coy elusiveness advocated by *The Rules.* The essence of its approach is playing hard to get: "Don't stare at men or talk too much." "Don't meet him halfway or go Dutch on a date." "Don't call him and rarely return his calls." Fein and Schneider are not recommending that a woman be cruel or crude — in this they would seem to be more high-minded than pickup artists — but what they are preaching is just as manipulative.

Why would a pickup artist use a neg? And why would he want to display an initial lack of interest in the target? Why should a woman using the Rules have to be so remote and disdainful?

The conclusion is obvious: behind these techniques lies a principle everyone else is using, for the most part unconsciously and therefore badly. The idiot in the Technicolor shirt is peacocking, the vulgarian bragging about his real estate holdings is demonstrating value, and the catlike indifference that women sometimes affect even toward men they adore is simply an application of the Rules. Indeed, Fein and Schneider make no claim to originality. "No one seems to remember exactly how *The Rules* got started, but we think they began circa 1917 with Melanie's grandmother who made men wait nervously in her parents' parlor in a small suburb of Michigan."[5] (Melanie is a friend of the authors who initiated them into this art in the early 1980s.) There is clearly some underlying dynamic here, one we are usually not aware of, even though we seem to hew to it like subjects of a totalitarian state.

One clue to the power of these strategies may lie in demonstrating value. "In other words," Strauss writes, "what makes me any different from any of the last twenty guys who approached her?"[6] What appears to be going on in courtship, not only in the gritty singles scene that is the sarger's domain but in the daintier world of Rules-based dating, is a fastidiously precise hierarchical ranking. You demonstrate your own value while downplaying that of your desired mate, thus implying that he or she would be lucky to get you and had better jump at the chance. The man does it by ostentation, the woman by remoteness, but the principle is the same.

People may wince at the idea that love might have a quantitative element in it, but it does. Anyone who has read a nineteenth-century English novel can remember how potential partners in those days were ranked by the amount of income and status they brought with them. Today looks are rated on a scale of 1 to 10 (the Web site hotornot.com is devoted to this pastime), and women sometimes speak of their boyfriends earning "points" (say, by making coffee in the morning or being extra-attentive to the woman's elderly aunt).

What constitutes value? Beauty, youth, health, social status, character, money, and intelligence, as well as a whole array of minor and often highly individualized qualities, ranging from a sense of humor to a resemblance to a movie star. Women have long cited the proverb "The way to a man's heart is through his stomach," although sometimes the route is by way of quite another organ entirely. Education is certainly a factor. A recent article in the *New York Times* about declining marriage rates for blue-collar men observed, "Many men without college degrees are not marrying because the pool of women in their social circles—those without college degrees—has shrunk. And the dwindling pool of women in this category often look for a mate with more education and hence better financial prospects."[7]

Other elements of value lurk beneath the surface of consciousness. In one scientific study, women were asked to smell men's used T-shirts and decide which they found the most "sexy-smelling."

The women turned out to choose the T-shirts of men with immune systems that (unbeknown to the women, of course) "were unlike but compatible with their own," according to Helen Fisher, an anthropologist specializing in romantic love.[8] (It's odd to reflect that it is precisely these "sexy smells" that we try so hard to rid ourselves of with scents and deodorants.)

These factors all vary wildly in individual preference. A man craving a large bosom may overlook a well-endowed woman's deficiencies in character or intelligence. A woman fond of the high life may forgive a suitor's advanced age or sagging jowls if she smells a fat checkbook in the vicinity. It's easy to be cynical about these calculations in the more extreme (and thus more comical) cases, but I doubt that anyone with any sexual feeling at all is totally free from them. Because this dynamic is so quantitative, I will simply call it the Equation.

Everyone knows the Equation. Children may seem oblivious to it, but they probably understand it better than they are given credit for; teenagers grope with it clumsily; sophisticated adults have a sharp eye for it and almost invariably know where they stand, whether or not they would be able to articulate the principle as I've tried to do. Although I don't know of any such formal concept in scholarly circles, the assumption of the Equation's reality underlies many academic discussions of sexual relations. Consider the following, from a recent book on marriage by the sociologist James Q. Wilson. Explaining how the "sex ratio" (the proportion of men to women) affects behavior in various societies, Wilson posits a hypothetical situation in which available men far outnumber available women:

> In such a world, consider Amy. If a man wishes only to have sex with her, Amy can, if she wishes, easily reject him for a man who is willing to marry her. And if the man wishing to marry her is less handsome, less intelligent, or less likely to be financially successful,

Amy can choose the rival. And of special importance to us, a man who does not seem prepared to support her child, should Amy have one, can be passed over in favor of one who is committed to matrimony and fatherhood.[9]

Citing a study by two other sociologists, Marcia Guttentag and Paul F. Second, Wilson describes how sex ratios are likely to affect social mores:

When there is a high sex ratio—that is, when there are many more men than women—marriage will be commonplace and cohabitation will be rare, women will play more traditional roles, and children will be raised in two-parent families. When there is a low sex ratio—that is, when there are many more women than men—marriages will be less common and more fragile, cohabitation will become more general, divorce will be more frequent, and children will be more likely to be raised in one-parent families. In the first case, women have a lot of bargaining power and so find it easier to get men to marry and stay with them; in the second case, women have less bargaining power and must settle for what they can get.[10]

So say the professors. To see how much we take the Equation for granted, consider an extreme exception. Say a beautiful twenty-year-old woman takes up with a street person—a decrepit old alcoholic who can't even speak coherently. What would anyone think? The Equation would be so wildly out of balance that her friends would gossip and her parents would probably try to get professional help for her. Her insistence that her disintegrating lover was her "soul mate" or "spiritual twin," no matter how heartfelt, would be taken as a sign of mental illness.

In most cases, those whose positions in the game of courtship are at wild variance rule each other out automatically. Many men find beautiful women intimidating. A homely man looks at a lovely woman and thinks, "I could never get her." For this reason, some even prefer a partner who is less attractive. Others may find themselves inexplicably charmed by a quirk or oddity. The great Japanese novelist Natsume Soseki said that what attracted him to his wife when he first met her was that she did not seem to be ashamed of her bad teeth.

Even the apparent exceptions don't disprove the rule. The playwright Arthur Miller was not conspicuously handsome, yet he married Marilyn Monroe, one of the most beautiful women of her time. Somehow this comes as no great surprise; Miller's brilliance and fame were a match for her beauty. (The marriage was evidently not a happy one, but the Equation has scant concern for happiness.) Sometimes people are indeed quite explicit about such trade-offs, as we see in the story about the actress who proposed a union with another playwright—George Bernard Shaw—on the grounds that a child with his brains and her looks would be a magnificent specimen. Shaw replied, "Yes, but what if the child has my looks and your brains?"

This type of calculation has long been recognized by theorists of love. The psychologist Erich Fromm, whose *Art of Loving* was perhaps the most influential book on the subject in the mid-twentieth century, writes:

> The sense of falling in love develops usually only with regard to such human commodities as are within reach of one's own possibilities for exchange. I am out for a bargain; the object should be desirable from the standpoint of its social value, and at the same time should want me, considering my overt and hidden assets and potentialities. Two persons thus fall in love when they feel they have found the best object available on

the market, considering the limitations of their own exchange values.

Fromm's use of commercial terminology is not entirely ironic. He goes on to say, "In a culture in which the marketing orientation prevails, and in which material success is the outstanding value, there is little reason to be surprised that human love relations follow the same pattern of exchange which governs the commodity and the labor market."[11] James Q. Wilson also speaks of "bargaining power" in relations between the sexes. Current slang uses similar terms: someone who is recently divorced or separated from a lover is said to be "back on the market," and bars devoted to the pickup scene are known as "meat markets."

One might object that while this kind of reckoning may be done by the more calculating members of humankind, it couldn't possibly apply to those of us who are more impetuous. How could the Equation explain love at first sight? Doesn't instant attraction happen far too fast for anyone to make this kind of appraisal?

Actually, the mind works faster than we may believe. In his popular book *Blink: The Power of Thinking Without Thinking*, Malcolm Gladwell explores what he calls the "adaptive unconscious," the part of the mind that makes split-second decisions. It may be the adaptive unconscious that's at work when we fall instantly in love. We may not be wrong to do so. As Gladwell explains, usually these judgments are better than those of the slower and more actuarial part that carries out conscious reasoning.[12] Gurdjieff too observes:

> Thought is too slow. It works out a certain plan of action and continues to follow it even though the circumstances have changed and quite a different course of action is necessary. Beside, in some cases the interference of the thinking center gives rise to entirely wrong reactions, because the thinking center is simply incapable

of understanding the shades and distinctions of many events. . . . Its decisions are much too general and do not correspond to the decisions which the emotional center would have made. . . . The mind cannot understand shades of feeling.[13]

Whether we call it the adaptive unconscious or the emotional center, this part of the mind has a great deal to do with what the psychologist Daniel Goleman has styled "emotional intelligence." On the other hand, the emotions are not infallible. As Goleman says, they are "childlike" and provide "a quick but sloppy response."[14] Gladwell too speaks of failures of blink. In love, we may make a split-second decision in the recesses of the unconscious, but we can easily be mistaken. We can also be misled.

To see how the Equation works in more detail, I'd like to turn to another expert on love: the nineteenth-century French novelist Stendhal. Stendhal's favorite of his own works was his wise and mischievous treatise *On Love*, in which he describes how love is born.[15] It begins with admiration; it is followed by hope: "One studies her perfections. It is at this moment that a woman should surrender herself, to get the greatest possible sensual pleasure. The eyes of even the most modest women light up the moment hope is born; passion is so strong and pleasure is so acute that they betray themselves in the most obvious manner."

In terms of the Equation, hope arises when an admirer decides he has a chance with someone he likes. Hope may be generated by a smile or a wink or by nothing more than the instantaneous calculation of one's own value compared to the other person's. Although the reckoning may not be accurate, in most sane people it must fall within some range of feasibility. A man may develop an effervescent crush on a charming actress, but only a psychopath tries to track her down.

After hope comes what Stendhal calls *crystallization*, which he defines as "that process of the mind which discovers fresh perfections in its beloved at every turn of events." Stendhal explains where he got this term:

> In the salt mines of Salzburg a bough stripped of its leaves by winter is thrown into the depths of the disused workings; two or three months later it is pulled out again, covered with brilliant crystals; even the tiniest twigs, no bigger than a tomtit's claw, are spangled with a vast number of shimmering, glittering diamonds, so that the original bough is no longer recognizable.

But, Stendhal continues, a man's affections "may still wander, for the spirit wearies of monotony, even in the case of the most perfect happiness." What rivets his attention at this point is *doubt*:

> If he takes too much for granted he will be met with indifference, coldness or even anger: in France there will be a suggestion of irony which seems to say: "You think you have made more progress than you really have." . . . The lover begins to be less sure of the happiness which he has promised himself; he begins to criticize the reasons he gave himself for hoping.

Doubt leads to the *second crystallization* in the lover, a phase in which "gaunt-eyed doubt grips him again and pulls him up with a jerk. His heart misses a beat; he says to himself: 'But does she love me?'"

Suddenly the logic of the Rules becomes extraordinarily clear. A woman who refuses to "open up too soon" or return her admirer's phone calls is simply making use of doubt. She is implying that she can do better than the man who is pursuing her—but not implying it so definitely that he gives up hope.

To see how this works in practice, we might turn to Marcel Proust's novel *Swann's Way*. The aesthete Charles Swann, introduced to the demimondaine Odette by a mutual friend, at first has little interest in her. "She had struck Swann not, certainly, as being devoid of beauty, but as endowed with a style of beauty which left him indifferent, which aroused in him no desire, which gave him, indeed, a sort of physical repulsion." Nevertheless he allows her to visit him on several occasions. "After Odette had left him, Swann would think with a smile of her telling him how the time would drag until he allowed her to come again; he remembered the anxious, timid way in which she had once begged him that it might not be very long."[16] Soon he finds himself looking forward to seeing her, taking her visits for granted.

The crisis comes one evening when Swann arrives at a soirée expecting to find Odette. Having driven another mistress home, he has come so late

> that Odette, supposing that he did not intend to come, had already left. Seeing the room bare of her, Swann felt his heart wrung by sudden anguish; he shook with the sense that he was being deprived of a pleasure whose intensity he began then for the first time to estimate, having always, hitherto, had that certainty of finding it whenever he would, which (as in the case of all our pleasures) reduced, if it did not altogether blind him to its dimensions.

The host remarks to his wife, "Did you notice the face he pulled when he saw that she wasn't there? . . . I think we may say that he's hooked."[17]

So begins Swann's downfall. A man of the highest culture and position, a friend of both the president of France and the prince of Wales, he finds himself toyed with and humiliated by a woman "who is not the embodiment of either virtue or intellect."[18] In the end, after innumerable torments, he exclaims,

"To think that I have wasted years of my life, that I have longed for death, that the greatest love that I have ever known has been for a woman who did not please me, who was not in my style!"[19]

Common sense suggests that doubt ought to lead away from love rather than toward it, but like the neg for Strauss's pickup artists, it seems to work in exactly the opposite fashion. Why? Why should "indifference, coldness or even anger" heighten the passions instead of squelching them? This makes no sense in terms of ordinary reason, but in terms of the Equation, it makes perfect sense.

By the logic of the Equation, each of us is trying to find a partner of the highest possible value, or, as Fromm puts it, "such human commodities as are within reach of one's own possibilities for exchange." So we aim for partners who are equal or slightly higher in value than ourselves. If they were much higher, we would have no hope; if they were much lower, we would have no interest. Too much eagerness is usually a sign of some disparity. "Discovering that one is loved in return really ought to disenchant the lover with the beloved," writes the German philosopher Friedrich Nietzsche. "'What? this person is modest enough to love even you? Or stupid enough? Or—or—.'"[20]

For Swann, Odette, a woman of easy virtue whom he initially doesn't even find attractive, begins much lower on the scale (as she is in both intelligence and social class). He permits himself to enjoy her as a mistress. The position is reversed only when he finds himself in doubt—when she is no longer to be taken for granted, when, in terms of the Equation, he is tricked into believing that she is of a higher rank than he is. This may be foolish on his part, but as we've seen, the emotions are prone to snap judgments of which they are not easily disabused.

The Equation also explains many other mystifying aspects of romance. Consider some axioms from the twelfth-century *Book of Courtly Love* by Andreas Capellanus: "The easy attainment of love makes it of little value; difficulty of attainment makes it prized."

Obviously, because in terms of the Equation, a partner who is difficult to attain is usually believed to be of higher value than oneself. "A man in love is always apprehensive." True, because he fears that his beloved could be captured by someone of higher value. "It is not proper to love any woman whom one should be ashamed to seek to marry." That is, a man is unlikely to love someone who is not reasonably close to himself according to the Equation's merciless reckonings.

Occasionally, the Equation even works when it involves someone an individual *would* be ashamed to marry. In W. Somerset Maugham's novel *Of Human Bondage*, the medical student Philip Carey is abused and tormented by the vulgar Cockney waitress Mildred Rogers. Like Swann with Odette, Philip is higher in social class than Mildred, and at first he doesn't even find her attractive, but he soon develops an insane passion for her. Her coldness and indifference certainly form part of her ironic attraction (the one who is less in love generally holds the upper hand), but the curious imbalance in their feelings is partly due to a deformity in Philip. He has a clubfoot, so he sees himself as less desirable than Mildred. Mildred exploits her advantage with a vicious cunning, taunting him as a "cripple" during their incessant arguments.

Instances of the Equation appear in many, if not most, works of world literature. Jane Austen's gentry rank each other with fastidious precision, not only by age and appearance and abilities but also by income and above all by class. Austen's novel *Emma* could be read almost entirely as a comedy of the Equation. In it Emma Woodhouse tries to find a match for her friend Harriet Smith, the bastard daughter of an unknown father. Harriet is pretty and well brought up, but Emma persists in overvaluing her, encouraging her first to reject the suit of a yeoman farmer named Robert Martin and then to pursue a match with Mr. Elton, the local vicar. Emma tells her friend Mr. Knightley that Robert Martin is not Harriet's equal.

"Not Harriet's equal!" exclaimed Mr. Knightley, loudly and warmly; and with calmer asperity added, a few moments afterwards, "No, he is not her equal, indeed, for he is as much her superior in sense as in situation. Emma, your infatuation about that girl blinds you. What are Harriet Smith's claims, either of birth, nature, or education, to any connection higher than Robert Martin?"

Mr. Knightley is as merciless about Harriet's prospects with Mr. Elton:

Depend upon it, Elton will not do. Elton is a very good sort of man and a very respectable vicar of Highbury, but not at all likely to make an imprudent match. He knows the value of a good income as well as anybody. . . . He is as well acquainted with his own claims as well as Harriet's.[21]

The plot turns out as Mr. Knightley predicts. After some misadventures, Harriet ends up with Robert Martin, Mr. Elton with a woman closer to his social position (though inferior in brains and poise; the Equation often requires certain trade-offs). Emma and Mr. Knightley wind up together—again obeying the Equation: the two of them are the richest and most eligible people in their district.

Leo Tolstoy's *Anna Karenina* offers an example of how the Equation expresses itself internally. Konstantin Levin, upstaged at a ball by the dashing Count Vronsky in his pursuit of the lovely young Kitty Scherbatsky, muses:

Yes, there's something unpleasant, even repulsive in me. . . . I don't suit other people. Too proud, they say. No, I'm not too proud. If I were proud I would never have put myself in such a position. And in his mind's eye he saw Vronsky, happy, kind-hearted, clever and serene, who had never, Levin supposed, been in such an execrable position as the one Levin found himself in that evening. Of course he is the one she would choose. And so she should, and I have nobody and nothing to complain of. I myself am to blame. What right had I to think she might want to join her life with mine? Who am I? What am I? A worthless creature nobody has any use for.[22]

Vronsky soon abandons Kitty for an adulterous affair with Anna Karenina, and Levin does marry Kitty. But here too, the couple, both of whom are noble and rich, are well matched in terms of the Equation, for all of Levin's pessimistic musings.

What, then, is the Equation for? The sociobiologists of our day would seem to agree with the philosopher Arthur Schopenhauer, who observed, "The ultimate aim of love affairs . . . is really more important than all other ends in human life, and is therefore quite worthy of the profound seriousness with which every one pursues it. . . . What is decided by it is nothing less than *the composition of the next generation* . . . the existence and the special nature of the human race in future."[23] By this view, the Equation serves the purposes of reproductive advantage. Each of us seeks the fittest possible mate, and satisfied or not, we settle for the best we can find. This is the law of nature, and the law is inexorable.

No one can deny that reproductive advantage plays a tremendous role in romance. It may even dictate the length of attachment. Noting that divorce rates around the world tend to peak around the fourth year of marriage, Helen Fisher speculates:

Perhaps . . . ancestral humans living some 3.5 million years ago paired with a mate *only long enough to rear a single child through infancy—about four years*. When

> a mother no longer needed to nurse or carry an infant
> constantly . . . , she no longer needed a full-time partner
> to ensure the survival of her child. Indeed, she could
> "divorce" a mate if she found a new man more to her
> liking.[24]

But reproduction cannot be the sole function of romantic love. If it were, no woman would ever fall in love past menopause, and homosexual love would not exist at all. Indeed, the nineteenth-century Russian philosopher Vladimir Solovyov, whose book *The Meaning of Love* remains one of the most profound and influential examinations of the subject, comes to the opposite conclusion—that the intensity of love has an *inverse* relation to begetting of offspring. He points out that if romantic love existed purely for perpetuating the species, we might expect to see some correlation between the intensity of love and its issue. But what we see is the opposite. Great loves frequently leave no offspring, and sound children are often born to people who have few or no feelings for each other.[25] Solovyov cites his examples from world literature, but if we want an example from history, we can take the romance of Britain's King Edward VIII with the American divorcée Wallis Simpson. Edward loved Wallis enough to give up the throne of what was then the world's most powerful nation for her sake, but they never had children. Nor did Dante and Beatrice, Napoleon and Josephine, or many of the other celebrated lovers of history.

Romantic love, then, seems to serve any number of purposes, of which childbearing is only one and often far from the most important. Human beings fall in love for a host of reasons—companionship, status, comfort, security, sex—that have little or nothing to do with engendering the fittest offspring. Even all these factors taken together provide only part of the answer. Would a man long for death, like Charles Swann, for mere companionship or sexual pleasure? What kind of status or security could

Philip Carey derive from Mildred? If such benefits made up the sum total of love's equation, unrequited love would be unknown: the one rejected would matter-of-factly go on to some less ideal but adequate substitute. But often this is precisely what does *not* happen. The spurned lover who pines away for the beloved, who insists, "I only want her" or "I only want him," even when other willing partners are at hand, or who commits suicide out of grief, is not acting rationally according to Darwinian theory or the Equation or any other logical explanation.

Solovyov provides his own answer to this question: "The meaning and worth of love . . . is that it forces us, with all our being, to acknowledge for *another* the same absolute central significance which, because of the power of our egotism, we are conscious of only in ourselves."[26] For Solovyov, it's not foolish or proud to recognize that we are beings with absolute significance—that I have value in my own right apart from any purposes I may serve. This is nothing more than the truth. The error comes with egotism: acting as if I were the *only* one in all the world with absolute significance. It is this error that romantic love enables or forces us to transcend. Romantic love is not universal love; it does not extend beyond one single person. But to go even that far is to step beyond the seemingly impassable boundary of one's own skin.

Solovyov is not naive about love even in this sense. He adds that this feeling of transcendence is fleeting and transient and in the end usually succumbs to the pressures of the everyday:

> The object of love does not in reality preserve that absolute significance which is attached to it by the dream of love. From the outsider's point of view this is clear from the very beginning; but the unintentional tinge of mockery, which inevitably accompanies the outsider's relations to lovers, turns out to be only the anticipation of their own disenchantment.[27]

Sooner or later the first flush of love—which is not an illusion but the truth, which sees the other as he or she really is, as a divine being of absolute value—fades away, leaving only a stale residue. For Solovyov, love in the true sense does not exist in human beings as we are now. "Love is as yet for humans what reason was for the animal world; it exists in its beginnings, or as an earnest of what it will be, but not as yet in actual fact."[28] Today's romantic love is to genuine love what modern man is to Nietzsche's superman.[29]

These reflections take us back to the main theme of this book, for here we can see the violent tension between the merciless Equation and the glimmerings of what I have called conscious love, which sees in the other the same "absolute central significance" that we ordinarily reserve for ourselves. But even these considerations don't entirely explain the excruciating urgency of romantic love. To begin to understand it, I might return to the definition with which I started this book: that love is what unites *self* and *other*. As Freud observed, "At the height of being in love the boundary between ego and object threatens to melt away. Against all the evidence of his senses, a man who is in love declares that 'I' and 'you' are one, and is prepared to behave as if it were a fact."[30]

Biology would seem to bear this out. It portrays the survival of the self—whether it is a one-celled organism or a human being—as an intense struggle to hold a hostile universe at bay. The organism must protect itself from things that would destroy it; it must also destroy things itself in order to survive. Wherever it looks, it sees nothing but enemies—either creatures that it must fear or ones by which it is feared in turn. Man may have raised up his institutions to offer himself some protection, but frequently these same institutions turn his fellow men into antagonists that are just as vicious. What is there to guarantee survival for more than a few instants to anything that has to stake out its existence in this way? The universe is sure to engulf and destroy it in an amount of time that is, by any objective reckoning, infinitesimal.

Even if the organism does manage to carve out some temporary space for itself in the universe, all it has achieved is a monstrous isolation. Like Cain, it is haunted by the sense "that every one that shall find me shall slay me" (Genesis 4:14). The loneliness is oppressive, not only because it is terrifying but also because it is false. The boundaries between the self and the world can never be utterly impassable; no relationship between the two could then exist at all. Thus no sooner has the self staked out its boundaries than it feels a contrary urge to go past them. For humans, the means of bridging this gap is often romantic love. Here, in the sublime and idealized *other* that is the beloved, the little self seems to have some means whereby it can preserve its identity while relaxing its hard-won but hideous solitude. If this is a false solution—and the speed with which love's spell passes suggests that it commonly is—it still seems better than nothing.

Sex also plays its part. The release from the self comes most powerfully at the moment of orgasm, the poor man's nirvana, the instant at which we in the ordinary state touch most closely upon transcendence. For that moment, no religious aspiration, no visitation from the realms of grace, is necessary. The self drops away, and one unites perhaps with one's partner, perhaps with something more universal. It may feel as if one's essence has somehow blended with that of the other. Such blending can occur even in the most transitory encounters, creating a strange disequilibrium. When it is all over, the two partners may spring apart, wondering whom or what they have joined with. This fact may explain the proverbial postcoital depression: "*Omne animal triste post coitum*" went the old adage—"Every animal is sad after intercourse."[31] The Roman poet Lucretius speaks of something similar in his haunting lines: "From the midst of the font of delights / Something bitter arises that galls in the joys themselves."[32]

Like love, sex cannot be solely for reproduction. Humans have discovered many uses for sex—reward, punishment, dominance, submission, commerce, intimacy, and, of course, sheer enjoyment.

To all appearances these uses will continue as long as the human race itself.

It's true, of course, that many social authorities try to enforce a close and indeed exclusive link between sex and love on the one hand and reproduction on the other. The extreme view, held, for example, by the Roman Catholic Church, is that God meant sex for reproduction alone and that any use of it for other purposes is reprehensible; hence the church's condemnation of birth control, abortion, and homosexuality. As we've seen, even this is a moderation of the church's position in its early centuries, when sexuality was demonized in practically all circumstances. In Chapter One I sketched out *how* orthodox Christianity came to take this position, but I didn't explain why. At this point, let me delve further into this question.

To begin with, any new religion must define itself against its competitors, both in doctrine and in practice.[33] The world that gave birth to Christianity had comparatively few sanctions against sexual expression. The pagan Greeks and Romans accepted a wide range of sexual practices, including extramarital intercourse, prostitution, homosexuality, and pederasty, as well as abortion and infanticide. And although the Jewish religion condemned many forms of sexuality, it regarded the sexual impulse itself as healthy and natural. Jews were (and are) expected to fulfill the Bible's first commandment: "Be fruitful, and multiply, and replenish the earth, and subdue it" (Genesis 1:28).

These were the positions staked out by Christianity's chief rivals. The Christian church had no choice but to take a stance in opposition to them, just as Christians had to choose another day for their sabbath than Saturday, which had already been claimed by the Jews. So from its earliest days, the new religion exalted celibacy and virginity above all other states.[34] Christ tells the Sadducees, "They which shall be accounted worthy to obtain that world, and the resurrection from the dead, neither marry nor are given in marriage" (Luke 20:35). Paul advises the Corinthians,

"I say therefore to the unmarried and to the widows, it is good for them to abide even as I. But if they cannot contain, let them marry: for it is better to marry than to burn" (1 Corinthians 7:8–9). And in Revelation, the 144,000 elders who sit before the throne of God are "they which are not defiled with women: for they are virgins" (Revelation 14:4). Unlike the heroes of the Old Testament—such as Moses, who remained sexually potent up to his death at age 120, or David and Solomon, with their many wives—the heroes of the New shunned sex entirely.

Furthermore, sexuality in the Late Roman Empire had become unusually degraded and degrading. We don't need to take the Christians' word for this; the pagan authors provide ample evidence. The historian Suetonius describes such lurid instances as Nero's affair with his own mother and the emperor Tiberius' *pisciculi* ("little fishes"), little boys whom he kept swimming around in his private pool to gratify him.[35] Messalina, wife of the emperor Claudius, became proverbial for her nymphomania. The satirist Juvenal paints the most graphic portrait of her antics:

> When the wife knew her husband was asleep,
> She dared prefer a mat to the Palatine bed.
> Donning a nocturnal hood, the whorish empress
> Departed, accompanied by a single maid.
> Covering her black hair with a blond wig,
> She went to a brothel hot with used rags,
> And entered her own empty cell. There, naked,
> With gilded nipples, under the name Lycisca,
> She lay down and displayed the womb that bore you,
>   noble Brittanicus.
> Agreeably she took all comers and asked them for their
>   coins.
> Finally, when the pimp let his girls go home,
> She was the last to close her cell,

And left unhappy, burning in her stiff, tense vulva,
Exhausted by men but still not satisfied.[36]

Such was the world that gave birth to Christianity. A reaction
was inevitable, and the Christians soon became as athletic in resist-
ing passion as the pagans were in indulging it.[37] The manifestations
of this new chastity proved strange in their own right. In the early
centuries of the new religion, some of its more ardent devotees
decided to test their spiritual strength. The men adopted *agapetae*
(from the word *agape*), spiritual sisters or wives with whom they
slept but did not have intercourse. The practice led, at the very
least, to suspicion. "From what sources has this plague of 'dearly
beloved sisters' found its way into the church?" Jerome complained
in the year 408. "They live in the same house with their male
friends; they occupy the same room, often the same bed; yet they
call us suspicious if we think anything is wrong." Cyprian, bishop
of Carthage, expressed similar views in a letter to a fellow church
leader, adding, "And do not let any of them think to defend herself
by saying that she may be examined and proven a virgin, for both
the hands and the eyes of the midwives are often deceived, and
even if she be found to be a virgin in that particular in which a
woman may be so, yet she may have sinned in some other part of
her body which may be corrupted and yet cannot be examined."[38]

What was going on? Contrary to the Lord's Prayer, the devotees
and their "spiritual sisters" seemed to be trying to lead themselves
into temptation. They must have succumbed at least sometimes.
Were they hypocrites, trying to circumvent the church's hostility
to sex by elaborate subterfuge? Undoubtedly some were, but there
are indications in the inner Christian tradition that something else
may have been afoot. Taking *agapetae* may have been intended
to achieve the much discussed but little understood process of
transmuting sexual energy.

The esoteric anatomies of many spiritual traditions place the
locus of sexual energy, naturally, near the genitals. Some say it

resides in what the Chinese call the *tan-t'ien* center, located in the abdomen some five fingerwidths below the navel; others say it lies coiled at the base of the spine, where it is known in Sanskrit as *kundalini*. The idea is to take this energy, which is often believed to be wasted in intercourse, and transmute it into a higher energy that can be used to attain illumination.

At its most basic, the process essentially consists of raising energy through sexual arousal and then sending it up the body to the heart or the head. In her book *Masturbation, Tantra, and Self-Love*, Margo Woods describes it in an autoerotic context:

> As for the masturbation exercise, the only thing to remember is that it is extremely simple—raising the body's sexual energy almost to the point of orgasm, and instead of letting the energy go out into the orgasm, allow it to come up in the body, up to the heart. It happens that, at the point just before orgasm, there is a channel open in the body, and if you rest at that point and put your attention in your heart, the energy which has been generated will flow naturally upwards toward the heart. You don't have to *do* anything; it just happens. Don't worry about what it feels like, or if it is happening, just do it! . . .
>
> You may have an orgasm at the end of a session if you like, or you may find that you come by accident, and that will probably end the session for you because the energy will be gone. Men particularly will need to stop each round far short of orgasm till they learn what the point of no return is for them.[39]

The Taoist teacher Stephen T. Chang describes a similar process that does not involve masturbation. A practice he calls the Deer Exercise involves raising the sexual energy by rubbing the *tan-t'ien* point while holding the scrotum (for men) or by rubbing the same point while also rubbing the breasts (for women), and then squeezing the anal muscles together while concentrating on "feeling a tingling sensation (similar to an electrical shock)" rising through the body.[40]

Various Taoist and Tantric practices are designed to raise sexual energy through intercourse itself. Chang describes a form of sex that he calls "Morning and Evening Prayers," so called because a couple is supposed to do them twice a day. The man and woman lie as still as possible, moving only so much as to allow the man to maintain an erection. "Then the couple enjoy and share the feelings derived from such closeness and stillness for as long as they desire. . . . The woman's orgasm . . . can last from two to twenty minutes. During this time, she is completely relaxed in a meditative state. Her body's tremblings and vaginal secretions are signs of orgasm." To keep from ejaculating, the man performs a Taoist exercise by which he sends sexual energy up through his body.[41] Tantra, too, usually involves some kind of delayed orgasm for one or both parties as a way of heightening ecstasy.

I can't offer any proof that the early Christian ascetics and their *agapetae* used any techniques of this sort—I rather doubt they did—but they may have been producing the same effects in themselves unconsciously or half-consciously. Two lovers lying chastely in bed may not have been attempting to circulate internal energy, but it could have happened nonetheless, and they might have felt it without necessarily knowing why or how. Something similar may be taking place when one feels chills going up the spine. This usually occurs when one is either frightened or experiencing a mild ecstasy, as when seeing a beautiful work of art or hearing a powerful piece of music—and, of course, when in the presence of one's beloved. In such cases, one may literally feel energy running up the spine to the heart or the head. Physical energy becomes emotional energy. Dante gives an exquisite example in his portrait of his love for the young Beatrice:

This marvel appeared before me again, dressed in purest white, walking between two other women of distinguished bearing, both older than herself. As they walked down the street she turned her eyes towards me where I stood in fear and trembling, and with her ineffable courtesy . . . she greeted me; and such was the virtue of her greeting that I seemed to experience the height of bliss. It was exactly the ninth hour of day when she gave me her sweet greeting. As this was the first time she had ever spoken to me, I was filled with such joy that, my senses reeling, I had to withdraw from the sight of others.[42]

Reading *La Vita Nuova*, Dante's autobiographical account of his love for Beatrice, one has the impression that in the end he does not want to marry her or make love to her or even be near her except on the rarest occasions. Not only is he content to admire her from a distance, but admiring her from a distance seems to be the point. To understand this, we must remember that Dante lived in the High Middle Ages, when courtly love, a strange and excruciating but highly sophisticated form of romance, was at its zenith. The name "courtly love"—*l'amour courtois*—comes from the fact that this practice was created and codified by actual "courts of love." Headed usually by a noblewoman—the most famous being Eleanor of Aquitaine—these courts made rulings and pronouncements in an attempt to create a kind of code for behavior in love. After the Middle Ages, remnants of this tradition survived in what is now commonly called chivalry.

Courtly love began with the admiration of a lady by a lover. He would first make himself known to her, gingerly and from a distance, and then would approach her and beg her to allow him to adore her. Sometimes he would subject himself to prodigious feats in order to win her favor. Ulrich von Lichtenstein, a knight of the thirteenth century, provides a remarkable instance. At the age of twelve, he chose as his lady a princess who was high above him in rank, much older than he, and, moreover, married. Initially Ulrich's advances met with no success. After ten years of admiration from a distance, he finally saw fit to approach her, but she rebuffed him, telling him he was too ugly to be her devotee. To please her, he had surgery—a painful and dangerous process in those days—to remove his harelip. After further trials, Ulrich rode from Venice to Bohemia, dressed as the goddess Venus, challenging knights to jousts all along the way. He was astonishingly successful, breaking an average of eight lances a day. At this point, the lady was more complaisant, though not much: she ordered him to appear before him, but in the guise of a leper. Finally she commanded him to go on a crusade. As always, he obeyed her, but before he left, she changed her mind and, after fifteen years, granted him her love. Ulrich chronicled these escapades in the *Frauendienst*, an autobiographical thirty thousand–line poem whose title means "the service of women."[43]

Courtly love, the theme of the medieval troubadours as well as endless scholarly studies in the centuries since, is in the end no less mysterious for all that has been written about it. The simplest way to understand it is as a kind of antimarriage. Courtly love was everything marriage was not. In marriage at that time, the man was the unquestioned superior; in courtly love, the man was merely a humble suppliant of *la dame de ses pensées*, "the lady of his thoughts." Marriage involved a legal commitment; courtly love could not take place between married people. (Dante was married to a woman named Gemma Donati, and Ulrich stopped off for three days on his epic journey to visit his wife and children.) An 1174 ruling by one of the courts of love stresses this point:

> We declare and affirm . . . that love cannot extend its rights over two married persons. For indeed lovers grant one another all things mutually and freely, without being impelled by any motive of necessity, whereas husband

and wife are held by their duty to submit their wills to each other and to refuse each other nothing.

May this judgement, which we have delivered with extreme caution, and after consulting with a great number of other ladies, be for you a constant and unassailable truth.[44]

In addition, marriage involved sexual intercourse; courtly love generally excluded sex. Not that it was always chaste. A man might love a lady from afar for years or decades without being allowed to approach her. When he did, their encounter might include the *assais* or "test," in which the lovers might touch, kiss, and fondle each other, possibly even bring each other to orgasm. But actual penetration was not permitted. The French scholar René Nelli writes, "The more meritorious the test for the lover, the more meritorious it became for her, and perilous to her honor."[45] No doubt the lovers fell prey to the perils more than once.

There is clearly some affinity here between the "test" of courtly love and the bizarre temptations to which the early Christians and their *agapetae* exposed themselves. I don't know of any studies that draw a connection between these two practices; the general consensus is that courtly love was created by the Cathars, the celebrated heretics of medieval Provence who sought to renounce carnality. This theory has gained remarkably wide acceptance despite the lack of any real evidence to substantiate it. The strongest argument on behalf of this claim is circumstantial: Catharism arose in southern France in the twelfth century, and so did courtly love; therefore, they must be connected.[46] In the end, however, there is something unsatisfying about this theory, not only because of the scantness of the evidence but also because it's difficult to connect the practice of courtly love with Cathar theology, which, to all appearances, was far too ascetic even to encourage such teasing encounters as the *assais*.

The theory for the origins of courtly love that I'm about to advance is, I must admit, extremely speculative. I am about to introduce twentieth-century sources as a way of explaining forms of behavior that go back a thousand years and more. Even so, I think the case should be heard.

Boris Mouravieff (1890–1966), an enigmatic Russian émigré who expounded what he said was the esoteric doctrine of Eastern Orthodoxy, gives a discussion of this subject that, though convoluted, casts a great deal of light on these puzzling details. Mouravieff deliberately invokes the courtly love tradition, speaking not only of *l'amour courtois* (he wrote in French) but of the "knight" and *la dame de ses pensées*.

Mouravieff's ideas go roughly as follows. Man, in his ordinary state, lives in a state of sleep submerged by his personality, that is, his conditioned ego. His quest must be to find his Self, his "real I," which for most of us lies buried in the unconscious. This search for the real "I" is the goal of esoteric work for a long time after one embarks on it. But when the aspirant discovers his real "I," he makes an astonishing discovery. This "I" is androgynous and bipolar, and it is not found in the aspirant alone. He must find his "polar being," the member of the opposite sex (and for Mouravieff, it is *always* the opposite sex) who completes his own being. "The great mystery lies in the fact that *the real 'I' of polar beings is one and indivisible*," Mouravieff writes. "One for the both of them."[47]

It is this polar being that for the "knight" is the "lady of his dreams." Mouravieff continues: "Only an infinitely small minority of human beings feel the anguish caused by their inward isolation and ardently aspire to find the *Lady of their dreams*. . . . This thought must literally devour the Knight's heart, forcing him to accomplish the most perilous feats with the aim of finding the object of his aspirations." Once he has found her—a process that is by no means easy, since a man can easily imagine that any woman is his polar being if she is attractive enough—the polar beings can be united "in their completed Individuality," which even "obtains absolute mastery over the body, producing powers which have been considered marvellous by human beings from time immemorial."[48]

What makes a couple polar beings? Mouravieff's theory is so intricate that it would take a book nearly as long as his to explain it in full. Simplifying it as much as possible, we might say that such polarity comprises spiritual, intellectual, emotional, and physical—that is, sexual—compatibility.[49] Any couple with all four of these has a situation that others might well envy; even many successful married couples may have no more than one or two. Moreover, compatibility doesn't always mean similarity. In some areas it does; in others it does not. Intellectual compatibility for the most part *does* seem to mean similarity. A pair of university professors are likely to be well matched in this area, as would another couple whose interests aspire no higher than NASCAR or reality TV. Emotional compatibility, by contrast, may be more likely to involve complementarity, one partner being dominant and the other more passive and submissive. Tradition ascribes these roles to the man and the woman respectively, but most people with some experience of life have a fairly clear idea of just how often this proves true in practice.

Otto Weininger, an Austrian philosopher whose magnum opus, *Sex and Character*, was highly influential in the early twentieth century, argued that no one is purely masculine or purely feminine; everyone is an admixture of both, and this admixture varies enormously from individual to individual. The key to attraction is that two people complement each other in their ratio of gender qualities. A man with three-fourths male and one-fourth female qualities would thus be ideally complemented by a woman with three-fourths female and one-fourth male characteristics. A macho male is best balanced by an extremely feminine woman, while an effeminate man needs a more masculine woman to complement him. Similar ratios prevail in homosexual relationships, Weininger adds. Although his formula probably doesn't work out in any exact mathematical fashion (which would be hard to calculate anyway), it does often seem to approximate what happens in life.[50]

Echoes of the idea of polar beings can be found in countless other places: in the *Symposium* of Plato, which presents a myth in which human beings were cloven in two by Zeus to diminish their power, so that each of us wanders around perpetually in search of the other half; in the Kabbalah, in which the sexual union mirrors the union of God in his transcendent and immanent aspects (the latter, known as the *Shekhinah* or "presence," is usually imagined as feminine); even in D. H. Lawrence, who writes in one of his novels that it takes a man and a woman together to make an angel.

Mouravieff, however, adds one stipulation that sets his perspective apart from the others'. He buries it at the end of the second volume of his compendious and difficult work. The union takes place through the "Baptism of Fire":

> The two lovers, conscious of their presumably integral polarity, are called upon straightway to renounce carnal love. They must do this consciously and of a common accord, at the same time cultivating the Sacred fire of their Love, which then takes the form of *courtly love*. . . .
>
> If the supposedly polar beings fall, this either signifies that they were not polar, or that they were not yet ripe enough for such an exploit. For them in that case, the *Great Chance* will be turned into a commonplace experience only a little more rich in meaning and colour than those before and after it.[51]

Mouravieff published his work in the 1960s, and I don't know of any sources before him that develop these ideas in the same way. Nonetheless, his account is striking for how much it explains of practices from centuries earlier, suggesting that Mouravieff may be describing a teaching that had previously been handed down from antiquity through the oral tradition. If the Christian devotees of love in earlier ages were operating according to a teaching like Mouravieff's, it would explain a tremendous amount of their behavior that is otherwise baffling—particularly why they seemed to be trying to arouse sexual energy without satisfying it.

Very little is known about Mouravieff's personal life, so it's hard to say how much experience he had with this practice. The most revealing account of courtly love as Mouravieff describes it—indeed, the only such account that I know of—can be found in a book called *Love Is Stronger Than Death*, in which Cynthia Bourgeault, an Episcopal priest and contemplative, tells of her passionate, though platonic, relationship with Rafe, a Trappist monk she met while staying at a Colorado monastery. The book is intense and, to many readers, disturbing; it has also caused some discomfort in the monastic community, for whom the book's unusual ideas and its relentless honesty do not always sit easily.[52]

For both Cynthia and Rafe, their relationship is a kind of spiritual experiment. In the beginning, it has many of the characteristics of the typical romance—the dance of intimacy and withdrawal, deep affection combined with misunderstandings and hurt feelings. But after eighteen months, it takes a remarkable turn when Rafe dies of a heart attack.

Rafe is laid out for burial in the "simple, stark, and haunting" Trappist custom. When the service is over, Bourgeault, against her own expectation, realizes that she is not going to leave. She sits all night in vigil over him; during this time, as she describes it, "there was nothing but love, a gratitude conveyed entirely through the skin, body to body, will to will. For that night I knew no sleepiness, no regret; it was the most profoundly luminous experience I have ever had. . . . And somewhere in those cold, dark hours, a voice that was distinctly Rafe's came to me saying, 'I will meet you in the body of hope.' "[53]

After Rafe's death, Cynthia feels her bond with him deepen—a bond that he himself had prepared: "From early on in our time together he became convinced that the purpose of our human love was to form a conscious connection that would survive his physical death, and to this end he bent his efforts." From her knowledge of esoteric Christianity, including Mouravieff, Bourgeault concludes that it is the "body of hope" that forms this conscious connection—a subtle vehicle that links the two even though one of them has passed beyond the grave, "a living, palpable, and conscious energy that holds the visible and invisible worlds together."[54]

According to Cynthia, the "sacred fire" of Rafe's and her love has formed a connection that fuses their identities, presumably for eternity. If the vows of conventional marriage are meant to last "till death do us part," those of courtly love seem to extend past death's gates. For Dante too, his love for Beatrice reaches into eternity, as she becomes his guide to the spheres of heaven in the *Paradiso*. Sexual love becomes spiritual love, and rather than furthering the reproduction of the species, it produces a higher form of immortality for the couple themselves.

As time passes, Cynthia finds that her contact with Rafe is very much present and alive. Once, in a moment of dejection, she is strolling along the seashore. Then, she writes, "I knew something was about to happen. The first thing I heard was Rafe's voice, out of nowhere (not an audible voice, but a strong inner impression), laughing: 'I love to see the water through you!' And then, to the heart of the matter, 'You don't have to come all the way to me, because I am also coming to you.' "[55]

Imagination? Maybe—but then much of what we consider reality is imagination as well. The proof lies in the relationship itself, and that can ultimately be known only to the couple. On the other hand, it is fair to ask whether every couple—indeed, every individual—must pass through this stage, as Mouravieff suggests, in order to attain the highest level of realization. If so, it is somewhat dismaying, as the love of Rafe and Cynthia does not offer much of a model for ordinary lovers in ordinary life.

That may be part of the point. Whenever I read of a truly great love, I am struck above all by its uniqueness. Such loves don't fit easily into conventional schemes. Chaste or carnal, blissful or ill-starred, they are in every case the deepest expressions of the individuals themselves. As the individuals advance into the depths of their own being, what they create is unique to them; it does not obey conventions or clichés.

Are such loves only for exceptional people, for the brilliant and the enlightened and the remarkable? Possibly, but it may be better to see the question in another light. The very thing that makes people remarkable may be their refusal to accept what Rafe calls "last year's language"—the preconceptions and stereotypes that we apply not only to others, but, far more disastrously, to ourselves. Perhaps every great love is like Rafe's and Cynthia's. It is not a journey, because a journey implies a terrain that is already fixed and preexisting. It is the creation of a new landscape that is like no other that has ever existed.

All this being said, it seems necessary to add some disclaimers. The notion of soul mates can be a dangerous one, and for many people it seems to be little more than a means by which the Equation can operate. It's extremely easy to detach yourself from a lover on the premise that you can do better. In such cases the imagined soul mate becomes only a mirage in the distance. Ethan Watters, chronicling relationships among sophisticated young urbanites, describes how this can feel subjectively:

> Like most modern singles, I wasn't just looking for a suitable spouse; I was soul-mate searching. Although I disliked the phrase's New Age connotations, I counted myself among the 94 percent of my fellow never-marrieds who, when asked in a Gallup poll, agreed that when

you marry, you want your spouse to be your soul mate first and foremost. Along with my friends, I discovered that searching for a soul mate wasn't so easy. Although I dated smart and charming women, the soul-mate standard I tried to apply was so elusive in my own mind that any disgruntlement could become a reason for the big what-are-we-doing? talk. I wasn't looking for that certain something, a friend once cruelly observed, I was looking for that certain *everything*.[56]

Then, too, what of the enormous numbers of people—single, divorced, or unhappily married—who have never found their soul mates? What of those of us who lead lives of serial monogamy? Or polyamory and polyfidelity?[57] Or prostitution? (The ancients in Babylonia knew that there is a sacred element even to this most despised and downtrodden of all professions.) All these types of relationship exist, have always existed, and to all appearances will continue to exist. Love is sometimes expressed in a bonding for life, sometimes in a brief affair, or occasionally even in a thing as transient as a one-night stand. Sometimes it is virginal, sometimes whorish. The theologians and psychologists don't like to admit such things, but they offer few alternatives except to define "real love" in a manner that is so rigid and circumscribed that they themselves often have trouble living up to it. By the standards set up by so many experts today, only committed, monogamous relationships count as "real love." Regardless of the experts' pronouncements, human love takes as many forms as imagination and feasibility will permit, and if it seems to break the rules on countless occasions, this only serves to remind us that rules are not gods.

As for transmuting sexual energy, although it can take place spontaneously and hence accidentally, in most cases conscious attempts to make it happen appear to fail. In fact, such transmutation was originally one of the principal reasons for practicing celibacy, but at this point it rarely seems to work. Those who abstain from sex on religious grounds are frequently not transmuting but repressing their desires, which can lead to mental illness of one sort of another—among which we can number bigotry, intolerance, superstition—or on the other hand to weird ecstasies that may amount to nothing more than psychic entertainment.[58] As one eighteenth-century physician said about the early Methodists, who were given to hysterical displays of religious enthusiasm: "I sincerely believe there are many methodists, more for the sake of those visions, new births, and holy overshadowings, than for a desire of serving and worshipping God acceptably. Many of them, I am sure, have a greater desire to get, than to be begotten; to generate than to be regenerated."[59]

For all of this talk of ecstasies and soul mates and sexual transmutation, it seems unlikely that transactionality ever totally vanishes from romantic love, even at its most exalted. At one juncture, for example, Cynthia wonders, "What is the point, particularly for Rafe, of continuing an open-ended partnership across the vale of death? For me the gains are fairly obvious, though by no means easy in day-to-day practice. . . . But what is there in all this for Rafe?"[60] Romantic love, even in its highest forms, doesn't remove the quid pro quo, although it may add a new dimension to it.

And what of those others, those who choose the more familiar path of marriage, usually considered the sine qua non of human fulfillment? It's to these that we turn next.

3

Conjugial Love

Y ou may notice an apparent mistake in this chapter's title. Shouldn't it be *conjugal* love?

As a matter of fact, this isn't a mistake. This strange usage comes from the works of the great Swedish mystic Emanuel Swedenborg (1688–1772), or rather from the translation of one of his works, *De amore conjugiali* (Swedenborg wrote in Latin). The title has been translated as *Conjugial Love*, and Swedenborg's followers (there are at least three denominations based on his teachings) still often refer to it this way, although more recent translations have styled it *Marital Love* or *Marriage Love*. The unusual word *conjugial* is meant to draw attention to Swedenborg's unique view of the love between a man and a woman.[1]

Swedenborg, one of Christianity's greatest visionaries, started out more or less conventionally. The son of a Lutheran bishop, he worked for much of his adulthood as a scientist and engineer, writing texts on subjects as diverse as anatomy, physics, and mining. When he was around fifty, however, he began to have visions of the unseen dimensions, including heaven, hell, and the realm of the spirits in between. For the rest of his life, he would expound on these visions, and the ideas that sprang from them, in a number of long and laborious texts that presented a radically new vision of reality.[2] I will return to other aspects of Swedenborg's thought later in this book; it is his views on "conjugial love" that I want to discuss here.

Although he was a great Christian mystic, Swedenborg was not a prude. It's likely that before his great religious transformation, he had mistresses in the fashion of European gentlemen of his day, and he was by no means opposed to the practice even afterward. In his characteristically cumbrous style, he writes, "In order . . . that the immoderateness and inordinateness may be curbed with those who labor with heat and for various reasons cannot hasten or advance marriage, and may be reduced to something moderate and ordered, there seems no other refuge or asylum, as it were, than to take a mistress, called in French *maîtresse*."[3] He also points out that brothels are tolerated "in populous cities" as a way of keeping men from committing adultery with other men's wives. Swedenborg even advocates concubinage in cases where there are "just causes of separation from the bed" between husband and wife, although he adds that if a man is sleeping with a concubine, he must not sleep with his wife at the same time: "Concubinage together with a wife is unlawful for Christians and detestable. . . . It is polygamy, and polygamy should be condemned, as it is, by Christendom."[4] He does not extend the same liberties to women; equality in sexual relations was not of his age.[5]

Swedenborg's attitudes toward sex were either remarkably modern or remarkably old-fashioned, depending on which direction one chooses to look, for, as we know, these practices have existed for ages and were frequently condoned far more than they have been in recent centuries. Nevertheless, he goes on to extol marital love, and he does so in a curious way, saying, for example, "Those who are in . . . concubinage for lawful, just, and weighty, real causes, may at the same time be in marital love." So, too, may be men who keep mistresses. As bizarre as this may sound, Swedenborg is in effect saying that while any number of expedients may be necessary in order to manage one's own desires, one should still aspire to marital love as an ideal. For those who, like Swedenborg himself, do not marry in earthly life, the possibility will be vouchsafed to them in heaven.[6]

Unlike many Christian theologians, Swedenborg doesn't regard marriage as a second-rate choice for those who can't maintain the high standard of celibacy; indeed, he argues that only marital love is truly chaste. "Chastity cannot be predicated of those who have renounced marriage, vowing perpetual celibacy, unless they have and retain a love for a true marital life."[7]

Why should Swedenborg exalt the marital state so highly? Not only is it "the fundamental love among all celestial and spiritual loves and among natural loves thence," but there is "a correspondence between this love and the marriage of the Lord and the Church."[8] Likening the relationship between Christ and the church (or in Judaism, between God and Israel) to the love of a married couple is not original to Swedenborg; it has long been a trope among esotericists and conventional believers alike. The Song of Solomon, with its vivid eroticism, was probably admitted to the biblical canon only because it was believed to allude to these mysteries.

For Swedenborg, the metaphor goes deeper. Practically the whole of his intricate theology is based on a fundamental polarity between the *true* and the *good*. The true and the good are, in his view, ultimately identical—"good and truth proceed from the Lord not as two but as one"[9]—but they are experienced differently, as *wisdom* (in the case of truth) and *love* (in the case of the good). Internally, a man has love at his core; wisdom proceeds outward from it. A woman is just the opposite. She has wisdom at her core; love proceeds outward from this. "This is an affection for loving knowledge, intelligence, and wisdom, yet not in herself, but in man." The union of man and woman, in genuine marital love, embodies the primordial marriage of the true and the good: "Male and female were created to be the very form of the marriage between good and truth." When this occurs—which, Swedenborg stresses, is rare in our era—the innermost parts of the couple's souls are opened, and they receive an "influx" of grace from the Lord.[10]

Here, too, Swedenborg echoes a theme that has resonated through the centuries. Male and female embody the primal forces of the universe; consequently, their union is a cosmic event. For the Kabbalists (whose ideas influenced Swedenborg), the male represents the transcendent aspect of God, while the female embodies the *Shekhinah*, the divine presence that is God's immanent aspect. Performed with the right intention, sex between man and wife is not merely indulging base desires. It is a means of joining the upper worlds with the lower. As abstract as this idea may sound, it has some powerful and perhaps bizarre implications. We, in our physical bodies, are the instruments not only for God's work in this world but for his experience as well. If our own consciousness is elevated during intercourse, our pleasure becomes God's pleasure as well. This may explain a cryptic remark by an eighteenth-century Kabbalist: "God favored me with a gift of grace, granting me understanding of the essence of sexual holiness. The holiness derives precisely from feeling the pleasure. This secret is wondrous, deep, and awesome."[11]

The Tantric tradition of Asia teaches something similar. Although Tantra is a dismayingly complex tradition to define,[12] some of its forms involve "the identification of each adept with the cosmic Shakti or Shiva," the primordial feminine and masculine, respectively. Some versions of Tantra enact this identification ritually in the *chakra puja*, or "wheel rite." In this ceremony, eight men and eight women sit in a circle surrounding a guru. They are paired off by lot, and after a ritual marriage that remains in force only for the length of the rite itself, they have intercourse. The Tantrist André Van Lysebeth writes, "An obvious question: why leave it to luck to match the couples? Why not let the guru do it? The aim is to put the ordinary man-woman relationship into question, a relationship that is usually held to be the most personal one possible. On doing this, possessiveness is non-existent. Sex becomes an impersonal force."[13]

Conversely, we might consider the possibility that the personal element in sexual love could be—is likely to be—little more than the result of the Equation's internal calculations. What we consider "personal" often amounts to the most superficial considerations: beauty, wealth, social status. Popular wisdom acknowledges this fact in the frequently asked question "What happens when her (or his) looks go?" Even when the personal element involves deeper aspects of character, it remains a treacherous ground to build on. Often the very thing that one at first loves most in another is later on the thing one comes most to hate.

To identify with a transcendent force, by contrast, is to become more than personal; it is to become an eternal and universal being. But does male-female love really embody the central mysteries of the universe? Homosexuals might have cause to quarrel with this view, and a conscious being from a species that had only one sex—or for that matter, three or more—might view things quite differently as well.

At this point it may be valuable to digress briefly to discuss homosexuality, now so pressing an issue in so many contexts. The standard points of view are the traditional one, which holds that homosexuality is unnatural and hence evil, and the more modern one, which holds that homosexuality is a natural variation about which there is nothing inherently sinful. Beyond a rather limited point, neither approach is particularly illuminating. On the one hand, if homosexuality is unnatural, why has it persisted so long in the face of so much opposition? On the other hand, if homosexuality is natural, what purpose does it serve? It would seem to refute pure Darwinism. If the whole game consists of reproductive survival, any genes that would predispose an individual toward sex without issue should have died out long ago. Even as fervent a Darwinist as Richard Dawkins (whose ideas we'll examine in the next chapter) concedes, "The homosexual phenotype [a physical trait determined by genetic instructions and environmental influences] seems to exist in males with sufficient frequency that it is something to give a Darwinian a bit of a worry."[14] (Dawkins does not explain why homosexuality in males presents "a bit of a worry" while female homosexuality apparently doesn't.)

The scientific explanations that have been touted include the "worker ant" theory: that homosexuals evolved to provide care for offspring, freeing up more dominant males for hunting; and the "sneaky gene" theory, arguing that since many homosexuals are actually bisexual, they would be able to gain the trust of a dominant male and thus insinuate themselves into his harem.[15] Both these theories seem preposterous. Even if homosexuals served as "worker ants," their genes would remain at a great disadvantage for survival because they would not be disposed to reproduce; and while the "sneaky gene" theory may conceivably explain bisexuality, it hardly accounts for exclusively homosexual preferences. The most obvious conclusion is that homosexuality seems to fulfill some function in nature that is not well understood. For the time being, we would probably be best served neither by condemning it nor by trying to cook up factitious reasons for its existence. I myself suspect that if the phenomenon were fully understood, it would show that there are other factors operating in evolution besides purely Darwinian ones.

From an ultimate perspective, there's probably nothing uniquely privileged about the union between man and woman. Nonetheless, for us as humans the dynamic of the two sexes does serve to symbolize one of the deepest aspects of reality—so deep, in fact, that it is both extremely important and extremely difficult to describe.

No matter what we may go through in life, two things inevitably accompany us. In the first place, there is something that *experiences*. In the second place, there is that which *is experienced*. These two forces exist, we may assume, in all things. It's not hard to conceive that animals, whatever their degree of intelligence, encounter the world in some such way; nor does it take much more imagination to think that some such consciousness, however rudimentary, could exist in plants and possibly even in the vast portion of the universe that is supposedly inanimate (an issue I'll discuss in Chapter Six).

In my book *Inner Christianity*, I discussed these two principles and used the terms "I" and "the world" to denote them, not only because they are the most common in esoteric Christianity but also because they connect us most vividly to the way we perceive these forces from instant to instant. There are other names for them as well. The "I" is also known as the Self; it is what the synoptic Gospels call the "kingdom of God" or the "kingdom of heaven," and what Exodus and the Gospel of John call "I am."[16] It is what is in us that is conscious. It can never be found, but it can never be lost, because it is always what is looking. Sometimes we may equate it with the ordinary, personal ego, but the spiritual masters of practically all traditions have always warned that this is a mistake. The true "I" goes deeper; in fact, if we begin to penetrate its nature, in meditation, for example, we find ourselves in an infinitely receding space. The Hindu sage Sri Ramana Maharshi said that the question "Who am I?" taken back far enough in one's mind could lead to enlightenment.

This "I," this Self, has some paradoxical characteristics. In sacred art and geometry it is often symbolized by a point (or a point in a circle) because it has no dimensions. Its existence often seems tenuous and faint. Because we generally allow it to remain undeveloped in ourselves, Christ likens it to a seed. It does nothing, but without it the world would not come into being, because there would be nothing and no one to experience it. Esoterically, it is the "All-Merciful," because it allows for and encompasses everything, good and evil, beautiful and ugly, painful and sweet. No matter what you experience, there will always be something that experiences it. Tradition holds that this is the only part of our nature that is truly immortal; the rest, being composed of our mortal bodies and our equally mortal personalities, will perish sooner or later.

This primordial consciousness has generally been associated with the masculine principle. This may seem arbitrary and even peculiar, because the "I" is in a sense strangely passive, a quality that's often ascribed to the feminine. It is ever-present, but it never moves. It does nothing, and yet without its presence nothing can happen. The same holds true in reproduction. After intercourse, the male does nothing; he has contributed the seed, and that is it. If the woman conceives, the baby will grow regardless of whether the man is present or not. In gestation, it is the woman who does all the work, but it is the male who has supplied one small, invisible, though absolutely necessary ingredient.

Esoteric teachings associate the primordial feminine with the "world," with all that *is experienced*, within and without, in all its manifold guises. This primal feminine, which gives rise to everything, is known by many names: the Great Goddess, the Divine Mother, the *anima mundi* or "spirit of the world," or Nature, whose name derives from a Latin root meaning "she who will give birth." Hindu philosophies such as the Samkhya refer to it as *prakrti*, which also means "nature"; Shakti, as we have seen, is a name for it in Tantra. It ceaselessly produces the world in all its forms, and it never stops producing.

To conceive of this force, imagine a kind of three-dimensional tapestry containing every experience you have ever had, good or bad, waking or dreaming, remembered or forgotten. Now imagine that this tapestry also seamlessly includes the experience of all other human beings that have lived or will live. It also includes the experience of every living creature on this earth—plant, animal, microbe, virus—and even of inanimate matter. Extend the tapestry wider to include the experience of every entity in the entire cosmos—not only extraterrestrial life in all possible forms but also the experiences of stars and planets and nebulae, of galaxies and universes, and of supernatural beings, of gods and angels and devils. Such is the handiwork, or the embodiment, of the Great Goddess, of the "world." It is infinite, or virtually so.

This tapestry, as inconceivably vast as it is, would not exist without primordial consciousness, the universal "I," the eternal Witness, to bring it into being by the simple act of cognizing it. Though we conceive of ourselves as individuals, radically isolated from the world, this belief is an illusion. Each of us is merely a localized representation of this universal consciousness.

Of the many myths that allude to this truth, among the most famous is the book of Genesis, which, as the sages have always known, is not a portrait of creation in any narrowly physical sense. Genesis begins with the "heaven" and the "earth." It *must* begin here because beyond this level nothing can be said. It goes on to say that "the earth was without form, and void; . . . and the Spirit of God moved upon the face of the waters" (Genesis 1:1–2). The text draws a parallel set of polarities: between the "heaven" and "the spirit of God" on the one hand—that is, consciousness—and "the earth" and "the waters" on the other—that is, the world. It is by this very polarization that being emerges from nonbeing, and the chaos of "the waters" solidifies into a palpable universe that is here called "earth."

Because, as it is taught, each of us is microcosm of the universe, we can observe a similar process in ourselves. In an undeveloped state of consciousness—which is what most people live in most of the time—the "I" and the world are not as clearly distinguished as we may believe. The "I" is identified with its own experience—its thoughts, emotions, desires, sensations. Immersed in its identification, the "I" forgets itself, an idea that is reflected in the Greek myth of Narcissus, who drowns when he falls into a pool while admiring his own image, as well as in the Christian sacrament of baptism, where one is ritually immersed in the waters of the psyche and raised up from them. To free the "I" from this identification is what it really means to be "born again."

Beginning to detach is the first step of the spiritual journey. It's usually an unpleasant process, for the same reason that it hurts to pull a strip of tape off one's skin: two things have gotten stuck together, and they don't always come apart so easily. In spiritual life, meditation is the classic means of unsticking consciousness from its own contents, but there are others: prayers, rituals, ethical observances. Despite these many tools, detachment tends to be an extremely lengthy process, so much so that few people, if any, totally accomplish it. The possibility always remains of becoming attached to a desired outcome, to a feeling or belief, to an image of oneself as an enlightened being, or even to a constricted and parochial notion of God. Mystical writings are full of warnings against this trap.

In any event, detachment creates a polarity. Here again we can see why the symbolism of male and female is so apt: the two things must be separate. But if the process stops here, everything becomes frozen in opposition. The next stage, then, is the mystical marriage, symbolized in remarkably similar ways in so many spiritual traditions. We have already looked at these ideas in Tantra, the Kabbalah, and Swedenborg. Alchemical texts and engravings of the early modern era—whose enigmatic and allusive quality suggests that they were concerned about more than the mere manufacture of gold—hint at much the same thing when they speak of the marriage of the alchemical king and queen, often represented in elaborate and enigmatic engravings. The product of this mystical marriage is the divine child, who represents the culmination of this perfect union between the male and the female, between the "I" and the "world." To emphasize the fact that the child has arisen from a union of the two polarities, it is sometimes depicted as a hermaphrodite.[17]

Understanding this symbolism casts a considerable amount of light on a great deal of mystical imagery, but what does it mean on a more concrete level? In cognitive terms, the divine child points to a new freshness and vividness that consciousness possesses after it has passed through the stage of detachment. It may seem contradictory to say that it is precisely the process of detachment—which we often associate with dissociation and deadness—that makes the world fresh and new. But it isn't as contradictory as it may seem. We often fail to realize how much we are blinded by our own agendas. They are filters that screen out much of the world from direct experience. Detachment is to a large degree separating and purifying consciousness from these filters.

A couple of anecdotes may help illustrate what I'm saying here. An old friend of mine who made a lot of money as an investment banker began raising beef cattle as a hobby. Once, as he was taking me around his ranch to show me his cows, I asked him, "Just how intelligent are they?" He replied, "When there's something they're interested in, they're remarkably intelligent." The implication was that apart from the few things that *did* interest them—food, water, sex, warmth in the winter, coolness in the summer—they were as oblivious as we usually take cattle to be. So are humans in more cases than we may care to admit. A man goes to a museum on a Sunday afternoon in the hopes of meeting a woman there. He goes, but he meets no one. From his point of view, the afternoon is a failure. His eyes may have passed across some of the world's great artistic masterpieces, but because this was not part of his agenda, he took no pleasure from them.

Such habits of thought may be especially common in acquisitive America. Not long ago, I found myself with some time to kill in a charming and stylish New England town. It was a beautiful day, so I decided to take a walk for a few blocks. As I went past the fine and extremely expensive houses, I began to calculate how much they must cost. I heard a voice in my head saying, "Try to look at them without price tags." I was able to do it, but it took a certain amount of conscious effort. And yet the effort was worth it. Freed from the habitual American agenda of viewing everything as a negotiable commodity, I was actually able to enjoy the beauty of the houses as they were, apart from their value as real estate. This at least suggests how detachment can give birth to a fresh outlook on life.

At the center of the Kabbalistic diagram known as the Tree of Life (which is a kind of rough schematic portrait of the universe, visible and invisible) is a principle called *Tiferet* or *Tiphereth*, which literally means "beauty." The reasons given for the name of this principle are many and varied, but it may be so called partly because when one is in the elevated state of consciousness associated with Tiferet, the world actually does appear beautiful. It has no need of fixing or healing; all is perfect as it is. One lesson of the profound spiritual text called *A Course in Miracles* says, "Let all things be exactly as they are."[18] John Wren-Lewis, an Englishman who had a spontaneous mystical awakening, writes of his experience, "It has everything to do with a dimension of aliveness here and now. . . . In fact it makes each present instant so utterly satisfying that even the success or failure of creative activity becomes relatively unimportant."[19]

The world's literature is full of testimonies to such awakenings. For all the sublimity of these writings, reading them can create a kind of detour, fostering expectations about this experience that can turn into an enormous impediment to it. (Wren-Lewis's awakening came to him unbidden, while he was lying in an Indonesian hospital, having eaten a piece of poisoned candy given him by a stranger.) This kind of experience is unlikely to resemble one's preconceptions, for the very simple reason that the preconceptions themselves are part of the screen that keeps it out. So rather than offering handy tips in the manner of a self-help manual, I'd like to suggest that this kind of awakening may be facilitated by contemplating two aphorisms, which are to be taken together:

The world is your body.

Do not take the world too seriously.

As a Tantric text says, "He who realizes the truth of the body can come to know the truth of the universe."[20] But knowing the truth of the body is not the same as identifying with the body. One leads to "the truth of the universe"; the other is a dead end that leads nowhere but to the deluded stagnation that we call ordinary life.

These thoughts offer some glimpse of what the ancient texts may be saying when they speak of the mystical marriage and the birth of the divine child. The practical-minded person may object that this is too rarefied and obscure; it has nothing to do with love in the real world. To that I could reply that the "real world" as we perceive it is for the most part the construction of our desires and agendas and has little to do with objective reality. Love is meaningless—and conscious love is impossible—unless we have at least some capacity for a fresh and immediate experience of the world. With such a capacity, we have a measure of freedom, some possibility of regarding others not as tools or mechanisms but as living beings like ourselves. In the language of the philosopher Martin Buber, "I" and "it" become "I" and "thou."

Having said all this, we might turn to marriage in its more familiar forms. In Christianity, one of the central texts on the subject is found in the Gospels:

> And the Pharisees came to him, and asked him, Is it lawful for a man to put away his wife? tempting him.
>
> And he answered and said unto them, What did Moses command you?
>
> And they said, Moses suffered us to write a bill of divorcement, and to put her away.
>
> And Jesus answered and said unto them, For the hardness of your heart he wrote you this precept.
>
> But from the beginning of the creation God made them male and female.
>
> For this cause shall a man leave his father and mother, and cleave to his wife:
>
> And they twain shall be one flesh: so then they are no more twain, but one flesh.
>
> What therefore God hath joined together, let not man put asunder. . . .

> And he saith unto them, Whosoever shall put away his wife, and marry another, committeth adultery against her.
>
> And if a woman shall put away her husband, and be married to another, she committeth adultery [Mark 10:2–9, 11–12; compare Matthew 19:3–9].

Of all the utterances ascribed to Christ, this has perhaps caused more needless pain than any other. John Milton inveighed against it in his 1644 treatise *The Doctrine and Discipline of Divorce*, in which he argued against a rigid and legalistic application of these teachings: "Our Saviours words touching divorce, are as it were congeal'd into a stony rigor, inconsistent both with his doctrine and his office; and that which he preacht onely to the conscience, is by Canonicall tyranny snatcht into the compulsive censure of a judiciall Court." Milton goes on to argue that "God regards Love and Peace in the family, more then [*sic*] a compulsive performance of mariage, which is more broke by a grievous continuance, then by a needfull divorce."[21]

Moses may have given "the bill of divorcement" for the hardness of the Israelites' hearts, but the passage of millennia does not seem to have softened the hearts of men and women to any discernible degree. Whether or not Christ is preaching "onely to the conscience," societies as a whole have had to acknowledge that the bond of marriage must at times be dissolved. The Protestant and Orthodox churches admit divorce; so, for that matter, does the Roman Catholic Church, although it has hedged the procedure around with the euphemism of "annulment."

Where and how, then, does the indissoluble bond of marriage arise? Christ's remarks appear to say that this bond is formed by the very performance of the marriage rite, or at any rate by the consummation, since presumably it is this that makes man and woman "one flesh." And yet the graft does not always take. In recent years, a marriage in the United States has had around a 40 percent chance of ending in divorce.[22] Such statistics are often trumpeted as signs of the moral degeneracy of our time, but is it really so? The British esotericist Dion Fortune, writing in the 1920s, says, "A statistician affirmed some time ago that in England 25 per cent. of married couples were permanently separated; 50 per cent. lived together without love, and 25 per cent. were happy."[23] The conservative British statesman Edmund Burke noted with dismay that in the revolutionary Paris of 1793, some 562 divorces occurred in the first three months, one-third of the number of marriages. Was this because the French Revolution led to "the total corruption of all morals," as Burke claimed, or because revolution now made divorce possible?[24]

If there are more divorces today, it's probably because the external pressures that formerly kept many marriages together have been relaxed. Divorce no longer has the social stigma that it once did. Furthermore, modern conveniences enable men and women to live alone much more feasibly than they could a hundred years ago, when even something as simple as washing clothes was an arduous task. Most important, a single woman today can earn a living on her own; she does not need a man to support her. A century or two ago, when there were few trades that women could engage in (and even fewer respectable ones), for a woman to live alone might have amounted to a death sentence.

There seems to be no truer an answer than to say that the bond is made, or proved, in the living. A couple start a marriage by swearing mighty oaths of fidelity before God and man, but they have no way of knowing whether they will be able to keep them. It is one of the great paradoxes of marriage that it entails a commitment of *feelings*. In the usual version of the vows, the couple swear to "love and honor" each other. One can make a commitment about one's actions, but can one honestly make a promise of love that will endure for the rest of one's life, through whatever unhappiness and misfortune may arise? Four decades ago, the psychologist Rollo May wrote a best seller called *Love and Will*, but how many of us have the will to enforce such discipline on our love? It is only through the lived experience that we know whether such bonds are really permanent and enduring. And today, at any rate, they survive not so much because of external pressure but because the couple have grown so close together that they find it unthinkable to be apart.

The Greek myth of Baucis and Philemon, an elderly couple who entertained Zeus and Hermes in disguise, beautifully illustrates this idea. Asked by the gods what favor they would like in return, Philemon says, "Since we have lived our years in concord, let the same hour take us both, so that I may never see my wife's bier, nor will she have to bury me." [25] Granting their wish, the gods transform them into a pair of twin oaks and their modest hut into a temple.

An enormous chasm, consisting not only of quantity but also of quality, stands between this love and a love that must be enforced by the constraints of society. While such undying, unkillable love is rare, it is not all that rare, and I—like many readers, I suspect—can think of a number of couples who fall into this category. It is a gift and a blessing as much as an act of will. While pop psychology insists that marriage takes work, a marriage that consists of nothing but work is unlikely ever to resemble the union of Baucis and Philemon. Marriage, like any relationship, *does* take will, but it is not the rigid stoicism with which we ordinarily associate that word. The Hungarian spiritual teacher Georg Kühlewind speaks of "the soft will," a mild, gentle way of directing one's intentions that does not arouse resistance or opposition. This may be the kind of will that "conjugial love" requires. It is not a matter of magnificent gestures or ostentatious vows; such grandiosity is alien to it. Rather it is proved and refined in countless small efforts of action and indeed of emotion, which can include anything from almost unnoticeable gestures of kindness to a forgiveness of offenses of which a more actuarial mind would make a scrupulous reckoning. The British physician Maurice Nicoll, a pupil of both Gurdjieff and Jung, called such calculations "keeping inner accounts." Few people, I would imagine, are entirely free of this failing, but if conscious love is to have any meaning, it must include the capacity to see these calculations in oneself and to deliberately set them aside.

Those who attain such heights may wonder if their union will last beyond the survival of the body. "Love is strong as death," the Bible tells us (Song of Solomon 8:6). Even in our brief investigations so far, we have seen this belief recur, for example, in Dante's reunion with Beatrice in the *Paradiso* and in the continuity of the love between Cynthia Bourgeault and Rafe after his death. This theme also surfaces in popular culture. In the 1990 film *Ghost*, a young man (played by Patrick Swayze) who is suddenly murdered comes back from the afterlife to help his widow (played by Demi Moore). The film ends with their parting, but the young man assures his wife that he will wait for her on the other side. Although the materialist dismisses such things as imagination, one might reply that it is their very persistence in the imagination that suggests their truth. Could we feel the need for love that survives the grave if the possibility did not exist?

Swedenborg, as we might expect, has his own intricate answers to this question. In his theology, the heavenly world is a continuation of this one. The angels (who have all lived as humans on earth) wear clothes, live in houses, do work, and as we have seen, get married. So a couple who have been married on earth do meet again in heaven. For Swedenborg, the journey through heaven is a journey inward: a man "comes first into his external self, and then into the internal." While the two partners are in the external state—that is, the more superficial aspect of their characters—they will live together in heaven. "But later, when they come into their internal state, the inclination becomes manifest, and if it is accordant and sympathetic, they continue their married life, but if discordant and antipathetic, they dissolve it." A man or a woman who has had several spouses on earth lives with each one in turn and then chooses either one or none of them, "for in the spiritual world, equally as in the natural, no Christian is permitted to marry several wives." Curiously, Swedenborg adds, "husbands rarely recognize their wives" in heaven, "but . . . wives readily recognize their husbands; the reason is that women have an interior perception of love, and men only an exterior."[26]

Whether or not we take Swedenborg's picture of the afterlife at face value, it is strikingly accurate as a picture of married life on earth. In the early years, it seems, the typical couple tend to live more on the surface; knowing someone in the deepest sense is not the task of a few weeks or months. It is only after a long and enduring time together that they can tell if they are compatible in the most inward sense. If, on the one hand, they discover they are not—which classically happens around midlife—one or both of them may begin to pull away, for reasons that they themselves may not understand. The relationship then either reconstitutes itself on a more authentic basis or ends in separation.

On the other hand, if the couple reach this level of inward compatibility, the marriage jumps a barrier that is as crucial as it is overlooked. Your spouse becomes part of your family. This does not always happen immediately, even in happy marriages. For years, perhaps, you may still think of your spouse as an outsider, as a beloved partner, perhaps, but not as someone of your own blood. Then there comes a point, possibly unnoticed at the time, when this barrier is passed, and your spouse becomes, as the biblical myth puts it, "bone of my bones, and flesh of my flesh" (Genesis 2:23). For some couples, this happens when they have a child, but this is hardly an infallible sign: for some, it happens before; for others, later or never. When it is reached, however, this is the point at which marital love passes into family love.

The Selfish Serpent

Mrs. March got her wet things off, her warm slippers on, and sitting down in the easy-chair, drew Amy to her lap, preparing to enjoy the happiest hour of her busy day. The girls flew about, trying to make things comfortable, each in her own way. Meg arranged the tea-table; Jo brought wood and set chairs, dropping, overturning, and clattering everything she touched; Beth trotted to and fro between parlour and kitchen, quiet and busy; while Amy gave directions to everyone, as she sat with her arms folded.[1]

Such was life in a mid-nineteenth-century American family as sketched by Louisa May Alcott at the beginning of *Little Women*. To this day the four March girls, with their mother and their housekeeper, Hannah, in their modest New England home, with their simple entertainments of singing and sewing and play-acting, seem to embody all that is good and sweet in domestic life. The Marches face darkness and sorrow: Mrs. March has to leave for Washington, where her husband, a Union Army chaplain during the Civil War, has fallen gravely ill; Beth too passes through a fever that brings her near death. Despite this drama, it is not the power of the narrative that has made this work a classic of children's literature; it is the portrait of a loving and close-knit home.

Indeed, no form of love seems more tender than the love we see in families. Few of us fail to be touched by a gathering of loved ones at holiday time, cozily assembled to enjoy food, gifts, and cheer, or by the recollection of a parent's kind attentions or a sweet, unpremeditated gesture of affection from a child.

If this were the whole story, family love would certainly be the purest of all varieties. But no sooner do these fond images flash across our minds than they are chased by others that are more forbidding: grim Christmas dinners silenced by a quarrel; brothers and sisters suing one another over a will; a grown child abandoning a mother in a nursing home. A father may tenderly comb the knots out of his daughter's hair today only to try to strangle her tomorrow.

The sublimities and vices of love between kin seem to be on a higher pitch than those of any other kind. Even more than with romantic love, the bonds between family members seem to be sealed by the demands of biology and the relentless mechanism of evolution. If we are to understand family love in any but the most superficial way, we need to take a look at these areas.

One of the most influential portraits of current evolutionary theory is Richard Dawkins's 1976 book *The Selfish Gene*. Dawkins, taking Darwin's theory of evolution into new terrain, proposes that the basic reproductive unit is the gene. Previously evolutionary theorists had thought in terms of individual or group survival, but for various reasons neither of these proved entirely satisfactory in explaining behavior in many species, whereas, according to Dawkins, the gene theory does.

As Dawkins describes it, life began when the primordial soup of inanimate protein on the earth four billion years ago produced, in some way that we don't understand, a strange mutant that was able to replicate itself. Consequently, "replicator" molecules were soon able to spread rapidly in the primordial ocean, using the abundant quantity of lifeless strings of protein as building blocks. This replicator molecule is the ancestor of what we today call DNA. (Dawkins suggests that it may have resembled viruses, which consist of nothing but strings of DNA covered with a protein coat.) Eventually, the lifeless protein became scarce, and the replicators began to use each other as material. Moreover, as the replicators made copies of themselves, small errors or variations crept in.

Here began the struggle to survive. Some of these variations, known as *mutations*, made the replicators better able to use other replicators as raw material—that is, as food; others enabled their possessors to defend themselves against being so used. As a result, these particular variations began to spread. Of course, there were other mutations that impeded the survival of their possessors, but these rapidly died out. Over the eons to come, the parry and thrust of the genes' drive for self-perpetuation produced the astonishing variety of life on earth. All of life, including humans, constitutes nothing more than a series of increasingly elaborate machines to ensure the survival of these replicating proteins.

"A predominant quality to be expected in a successful gene is ruthless selfishness," Dawkins argues. "This gene selfishness will usually give rise to selfishness in individual behavior. However, . . . there are special circumstances in which a gene can achieve its own selfish goals best by fostering a limited form of altruism at the level of individual animals."[2] Here Dawkins is drawing on the work of the sociobiologist Robert L. Trivers, who has argued that most, if not all, forms of altruism that we see in nature can be explained this way. An animal will invest time and energy in its child, who possesses half of its genes (the child receiving half its genes from the mother and half from the father). A parent may even sacrifice itself for its child. Why? Because the child is obviously younger than the parent and, all else being equal, has a greater chance of perpetuating its genes into the future.

Dawkins frequently sounds as if the genes themselves have a conscious purpose—selfishness and so on. The British philosopher Mary Midgley chides him for his "habitual rhetoric in elevating the gene from its real position as a humble piece of goo within cells to a malign and all-powerful agent."[3] But Dawkins stresses that he is not attributing consciousness to genes; it is merely a manner of speaking. There is no conscious purpose as such. The selfish genes replicate themselves blindly; it is survival alone that dictates which will prevail.

Even from this sketchy portrait, it's clear why this version of Darwinism throws religious believers into consternation. There is no need for a creator God here, nor is there room for one. The whole theory simply starts with proteins that have some drive to replicate themselves, a feature that they share to some degree with inanimate structures such as crystals. (Some biologists have suggested that originally clay crystal structures may have formed a kind of bridge between inanimate matter and life as we know it.) Moreover, the Darwinian world is a terribly vicious and amoral one. There are no rules of fair play. The selfish genes have no qualms about stealing, cheating, lying, and killing to survive. Cuckoos, for example, are well known for laying their eggs in the nests of other species. There is one species of cuckoo in which the hatching chick immediately hacks all the other chicks in the nest to pieces.

It may come as a surprise, then, when I say that I see no contradiction between this theory and esoteric doctrine as I understand it. Remember that in esoteric terms, we began with nothing more than "I" and "the world": *self* and *other*. Moreover, as I said, this sense of "I," this consciousness, exists in all things. Dawkins's genes are blind and unreasoning, but even they must possess a rudimentary capacity to know that they exist against and apart from a world so that they may try to attain a weird pseudo-immortality through reproduction.

The Kabbalah has a name for this drive. It is *netzach* (a Hebrew word that is also transliterated as *nezah* or in other forms). The usual translation is "eternity," but this is not really accurate. *Netzach* means something closer to "perpetuation" or perhaps even "inertia"—the tendency of something in motion to continue in motion. Kabbalists associate this principle with the cycles of nature, sex, and reproduction. It is as mechanical as a bicycle wheel that keeps on spinning until it runs out of energy.

Where, then, is God? In trying to understand this, we need to recognize that there are (at least) two different meanings of the term *God*. For as far back in history as we can see, the term *God* has been used in a very familiar but often overlooked sense—as the cause of things in the world whose causes we do not understand. When people didn't know what produces thunder or lightning or other natural phenomena, they attributed these things to God or the gods. As science became more adept at finding natural explanations for these phenomena, God in this sense became increasingly irrelevant. For this reason science has generally been regarded (and has regarded itself) as atheistic or agnostic. In recent years Dawkins himself has become a militant spokesman for atheism.

The use of God as a kind of causal last resort is very dubious, and science has been right to be skeptical of it. But there is another sense in which the concept of God is *not* meaningless: it is as the powerful force (or, if you prefer, person) that we experience as the source of our own being and indeed of all existence. This God does not need to be hypothesized or taken as a matter of faith; it is a matter of living experience, of what the theologian Rudolf Otto called the *mysterium tremendum et fascinans*, the "terrifying and attractive mystery." The overwhelming number of people in all ages and cultures and locations who have had knowledge of this power and given it their own names and clothed it in their own images is verification enough. God in this sense is not identical to what I have called the principle of "I" or consciousness, but this "I" is, in a sense, the forecourt to the knowledge of God. That is the mystical meaning of Christ's saying "I am the door" (John 10:9): The "I" is the door.

God, then, is not a furtive inventor tinkering with the workings of the world. Rather God is what is behind us; God underlies all reality, the reality even of "I" and "the world." It is in this way that God is the creator of heaven and earth. This is what the Kabbalists mean when they speak of the *Ain Sof*, the "infinite," and what the medieval mystic Meister Eckhart called the Godhead. As these sages have insisted, nothing can be said about God in this ultimate sense. Strictly speaking, one cannot even say that God is unknowable, because even saying that is to make a limiting statement about what cannot be limited.

If this is so, where does God stand in relation to evolution? Is evolution a kind of cosmic mechanism set into operation by God, who afterward stepped back to watch the show? (The theological term for this concept is *deus otiosus*, the "lazy God" who does nothing after creation.)

One compelling line of thought about this issue appears in a work called *Meditations on the Tarot*, which, although it was published in English only a little over twenty years ago, has already become a classic of esoteric Christianity. It was published anonymously and posthumously, at the author's request, but we now know that it was written by Valentin Tomberg (1900–1973), an esotericist born in Russia who was raised as a Lutheran, became a disciple of the Austrian spiritual teacher Rudolf Steiner, and ended his life as a Roman Catholic.[4] Tomberg's views on evolution are worth quoting at length:

> It is the *method* of so-called natural evolution which has replaced since the Fall the world created by God (i.e., "paradise"). Because evolution proceeds gropingly from form to form, trying and rejecting, then trying anew . . . the world of evolution from protozoa to vertebrates and from vertebrates to mammals and then to apes and to *pithecanthropus* is neither the accomplishment of absolute wisdom nor absolute goodness. It is rather the work of a really vast intelligence and a very resolute will pursuing a definite aim determined by the method of "trial

and error." One could say that it is a matter more of a great scientific intellect and the will of an experimenter which is revealed in natural evolution (the existence of which one can no longer deny), rather than divine wisdom and goodness. The tableau of evolution that the natural sciences—above all biology—have at last obtained as the result of prodigious work reveals to us *without any doubt* the work of a very subtle, but imperfect, intellect and a very determined, but imperfect, will. It is therefore the serpent, "the most artful animal of the fields," that the world of biological evolution reveals to us, and not God. It is the serpent who is the "prince of this world," and who is the author and director of the purely biological evolution following the Fall.[5]

Here we are very far from naive conceptions of a clockmaker God or intelligent design. A materialist like Richard Dawkins would indubitably quarrel with Tomberg's conception of a "very subtle, but imperfect, intellect," preferring to regard the process as the play of blind forces. One could ask why even highly mechanistic portraits of biological behavior somehow cannot shake the metaphor of consciousness. Regardless, the outcome is the same. The universe as we know it, including evolution and the replications of the selfish gene, is not the creation of God but is a consequence of the Fall.

The Fall, in esoteric Christian terms, is quite different from the way it's usually imagined. In the conventional view, God got mad at the human race because our primordial parents ate a piece of fruit, so he cast them out of the pretty park he had designed for them. At this point no intelligent person can take this story at face value. But as a mythic view of the human condition, the Genesis account remains profoundly true.[6]

To eat of the "tree of knowledge of good and evil" is not to take a bite from an apple. It is to know good and evil—and this can only be done by experiencing them directly. In essence, the Genesis story is saying that originally the human race was not intended to experience good and evil as we face them on this earth. Humanity was intended to inhabit a different, happier realm, which is entirely outside of the realm of nature as we know it. But humanity decided to experience reality in *this* form, and this has caused all the suffering as well as all the joy known throughout the ages.

Esoterically speaking, this decision, this Fall, took place outside the time line of history, even of natural history. There is no point in the physical past to which we can go back and find a time of primordial innocence and happiness. If primitive life was innocent, it was also, as anthropologists stress, vicious, uncertain, and fraught with terror. All of natural history, dating from the Big Bang or possibly even before that, is the result of this desire to experience good and evil, which, according to Christianity, was contrary to the Creator's original intent.

This view is likely to seem simplistic and anthropocentric in its own right. All the universe, then, is the result of some *human* decision on another plane of reality? Yes and no. The Genesis myth is a myth. It is intended for humans, so it's necessarily going to be anthropocentric. Consequently, we can't take even this esoteric explanation totally at face value as a picture of reality, particularly since reality as we know it, including the laws of time and space and causality, is the result of this Fall. We might, however, push the myth further and say that the Fall was the result of a decision by all of consciousness, all of what we now call *life*—or still further, all of what we now call *existence*—to know good and evil at this level of reality. If this were so, it would go far toward explaining birth and survival and death as they manifest themselves in the lives of stars and men and microbes.

What preceded the Fall is as mysterious as what preceded the Big Bang (although I would be reluctant to draw any explicit connection between the two). When nature, the universe, and everything in it, including the deepest structures of time, space, and causality, are a consequence of a tremendous cosmic rupture, what could we say about the realm that preceded it? We cannot make any accurate analogies for it, because any analogy we could make would come from the world we know, which is itself the result of the Fall.

Esotericists have thus had to resort to myth and symbolism to describe these concepts. The sixteenth-century Kabbalist Isaac Luria called this primordial disaster the *shevirat ha-kelim*, the "shattering of the vessels" that were created to, but could not, contain the divine light. The vessels broke, flinging the sparks of light in all directions, a condition from which the pious Jew has to redeem them by conscious performance of the commandments of the Law. Another version of this idea appears in *A Course in Miracles*, which says that the world we see is the result of the "separation," a decision by the collective Son of God, which includes all of us, to imagine himself as apart from the Father, our true source. The *Course* refers to this desire to be separate as the *ego*. Conventional Christianity calls it the Devil and equates it with the serpent of Genesis, tempting Adam with the knowledge of good and evil.

Why should the serpent have the sinister honor of personifying this malevolent force? Many answers have been given, but it's interesting to note that the strands of DNA are long and thin—serpentine. Could this horror of the serpent come from some recollection, so deeply embedded that it goes back before the genesis of the human race, that in practically all of what we call life, these serpentine strands of protein, clever and vicious, are what binds our consciousness to matter, binds the "I" to the "world," in a way that God did not intend? Could the serpent of Genesis be our own DNA?

In his book *The Cosmic Serpent: DNA and the Origins of Knowledge*, the anthropologist Jeremy Narby explores a similar idea. While investigating South American shamanism, Narby drank the psychedelic beverage known as ayahuasca. Ayahuasca, nicknamed the "television of the jungle," induces powerful visions of carnivals of spirits, luminous animals, and bizarre alternative realities. Narby also discovered, both in his own experience and in descriptions of others' visions, that among the most common visions were those of enormous fluorescent serpents: "People who drink ayahuasca see colorful and gigantic snakes more than any other vision."[7] (I myself have drunk ayahuasca twice and must admit that I didn't see snakes or for that matter much of anything at all, experiencing only in a profoundly visceral sense the truth that ayahuasca was not for me; nevertheless, I'm willing to believe Narby on this point.) Exploring the symbolism of the serpent in many cultures worldwide, he found that it had a cosmic significance—the most familiar being the *ouroboros*, the tail-eating serpent that serves as a symbol of eternity.

"I went on," Narby writes, "to look for the connection between the cosmic serpent—the master of transformation of serpentine form that lives in water and can be both extremely long and small, single and double—and DNA. I found that DNA corresponds exactly to this description." For Narby, as for Tomberg, the serpent is the quintessential symbol of life on earth (although Narby does not mention the Genesis myth). Unlike Tomberg, however, Narby draws an explicit connection between this serpent and DNA. He suggests:

> In their visions, shamans take their consciousness down to the molecular level and gain access to information related to DNA, which they call "animate essences" and "spirits." This is where they see double helixes, twisted ladders, and chromosome shapes. This is how shamanic cultures have known for millennia that the vital principle is the same for all living beings and is shaped like two entwined serpents (or a vine, a rope, a ladder . . .).[8]

Of course, Narby also has to concede that since the serpent symbol appears in many cultures that do not use psychedelic plants, there must be many ways of gaining access to this level of consciousness.

Narby observes that the serpent has a highly ambiguous nature in many of these myths. It is powerful and sublime, but it is also dreadful in the old sense of the term: it evokes dread. The serpent is "life-creating" and "knowledge-imparting," but it is also terrifying. Why? Narby (correctly, in my view) dismisses reductionistic answers that are based simply on the fact that some snakes are poisonous (he points out that many of the most venerated snakes are not poisonous),[9] but he doesn't really deal with the serpent's dual nature: it is as much feared and reviled as it is admired. Nevertheless, the answer to this puzzle seems reasonably clear. The "serpent"—the strands of DNA that serve as the core of life—binds this life to suffering and death as well as to joy. Neither exists without the other. Narby writes at length about the symbolism, also universal, of twin intertwined serpents (as in the caduceus) and connects them with the double helix of DNA, but one could add that the twins also symbolize good and evil or anguish and delight, which are inextricably paired as well.

To return to the Genesis myth, we might go back and recollect the punishment God visits upon the primordial couple. It is not hell or damnation; actually, it's rather mundane. To the woman God says, "In sorrow thou shalt bring forth children." To the man he says, "In the sweat of thy face shalt thou eat bread, till thou return unto the ground" (Genesis 3:16, 19). The punishment is consignment to the world we know, where it hurts to have babies and we have to work hard to make a living. All of life is subject to the same constraints. The lilies of the field toil not, neither do they spin, but no doubt photosynthesis and pollination are hard enough for them.

The Fall is thus a cosmic event. It involves all of life as we know it: "For we know that the whole creation groaneth and travaileth in pain together until now" (Romans 8:22). Although the Bible presents the situation in anthropocentric terms—it is all the fault of the cosmic man and woman—we have to bear in mind that all sacred teaching is of necessity directed to us as humans and will focus on humans. A truly cosmic perspective might show the matter quite differently—but is any of us capable of a truly cosmic perspective, of seeing totally past the limits of human perception?

"In the sweat of thy face shalt thou earn thy bread, till thou return to the ground; for out of it thou wast taken: for dust thou art, and unto dust shalt thou return." The author of this passage may have been the first writer in history to connect the concepts of work and death, but he was not the last. The psychologist Norman O. Brown remarks, "There is no way of defining work, as distinct from enjoyable effort, except as effort spent in fighting death." Brown quotes John Ruskin, who wrote that work is "that quantity of our toil which we die in."[10]

Work and birth, life and death. These are the horizons of our experience as living creatures. If the situation were totally natural, totally right, it is hard to imagine that we would feel as much discomfort with it as we do. Is our longing for another, better world mere delusion, or does it represent an insight deep within the human heart that no amount of rhapsodizing about the beauty of nature can entirely eradicate? God cannot be both all-good and all-powerful, the philosophers tell us. But he *could* be both—if this world were not his creation but rather a flight from his creation.

These ideas are disturbing, and most conventional theologians have been uncomfortable with them. The usual picture has been a somewhat childish one: the primordial Eden was a kind of nature preserve in which lions literally lay down with lambs. Through the Fall, as the old axiom put it, *natura vulnerata, non deleta*—"nature was wounded but not destroyed." The lions did not change shape, but they did start to eat the lambs. Unfortunately, science has made it impossible to take this view seriously. Nature, as far back as we can see, has always been as it is. It has neither been wounded nor destroyed; it simply marches on blindly as it will.

The ideas that I'm proposing here, by contrast, do not contradict science. Because they place the cosmic tragedy of the Fall in a totally different realm and on a totally different scale, they leave science to draw whatever conclusions it likes about the physical world. This theory thus takes away the burden of cramming scientific findings into a theological box. At the same time, it also frees us from the despair that may arise out of pure materialism. If there is a Fall, there must also be a redemption—but this must be a redemption that takes place outside of time or, to use traditional language, that brings about "the end of time." The end of time would also imply the end of space, quantity, causation, and the other fundamental matrices of reality as we know them.

The implications of these ideas are vast, and it would outstrip my purpose (and perhaps my capacities) to go into them further here. But I felt it necessary to make this digression in order to show that family love, the love that is programmed into our genes and makes us steal and kill for our offspring, is not conscious or unconditional love. On the contrary: it is highly unconscious and highly conditional. Many parents to whom I've mentioned this possibility strenuously disagree. Up to a point they are right. One loves one's child no matter what he or she may do or become. But is this unconditional love? No. It is totally conditional on the fact that this person is your child. André Van Lysebeth writes:

> Let's take the most "personal" love possible, that of a mother's love for her child. First, we should remember that this love does not always exist at birth: in many cases it comes only a few days later, when the newborn child begins to suck his mother's breasts. In fact, it is pure luck if this one baby is born at all. If, out of the hundreds of millions of spermatozoa, the ovum had been impregnated by another, this mother would have had quite another baby. Whichever sperm succeeds, the resulting baby is still loved by the mother in the same "personal" way.[11]

The tender and fierce love of a mother for her baby is not the love that comes from God but the love that comes from the serpent, from life's fervent and often vicious desire to perpetuate itself. This is not a moral judgment but simply a statement of biological fact. As Richard Dawkins reminds us, if the selfish strings of protein had operated differently, they would not have perpetuated themselves to this day.

Accepting all this may be difficult, and accepting it, moreover, as a *Christian* perspective may seem like far too much to swallow. But is it? If it were so, it would explain a baffling thing about the Gospels. Over and over they portray Christ as having practically no respect for family love. Unlike certain evangelical Christians, he is no advocate of "family values," and he usually shows little respect for his own family. When his mother at the feast at Cana tells him the wine is gone, he contemptuously replies, "Woman, what have I to do with thee?" (John 2:4). When told that his mother and brothers are waiting for him outside, he says, "Whosoever shall do the will of my Father which is in heaven, the same is my brother, and sister, and mother" (Matthew 12:50). Most shockingly, he says, "If any man come to me, and hate not his father, and mother, and wife, and children, and brethren, and sisters, yea, and his own life also, he cannot be my disciple" (Luke 14:26).

Taking these utterances at face value, we might conclude that Christ was simply a cult leader who wanted his followers to break off all their other connections. But we may be able to see a deeper side to the matter. Christ may in effect be saying that if we really are to attain the highest dimension of love, known as "everlasting life," we are going to have to go past, even at times rid ourselves, of what we normally conceive of as love, including our bonds with our nearest kin.

You may be aghast at what I seem to be suggesting. Ridding ourselves of family love? Mother love, the most sacrosanct of human impulses, as the product of the serpent? Such contentions seem cynical and harsh. They may be both, but they raise an issue that needs to be addressed before we go further. We cannot speak about conscious love without being ruthlessly honest about our own motives. Our idealizations of parental love may be nothing more than covers thrown over the machinations of our merciless genes. These thoughts are disquieting, but I believe that if we are to penetrate to love in its deepest sense, we have to face them. Thomas Merton observes:

> Before we can realize who we really are, we must become conscious of the fact that the person we think we are, here and now, is at best an impostor and a stranger. We must constantly question his motives and penetrate his disguises. Otherwise our attempts at self-knowledge are bound to fail, for if we fully and complacently acquiesce in our own illusion of who we are, our "self-knowledge" will only strive to reinforce our identification of ourselves with this impostor.[12]

This point needs to be stressed in contemporary America, which has an eerie propensity to paste smiling faces over everything while tens of millions of its citizens are suffocating with anxiety and depression. Most of the books written on love in recent decades are, to one degree or another, laced with this artificial sweetness. They have provided cake frosting in place of solid food. There is no point in writing another such book.

To return to the subject at hand: in Chapter Three, I suggested that part of the function of romantic love is to enable the individual to transcend herself, to go past the boundaries of her own being, if only for the second or two that orgasm usually lasts. Parental love has a different thrust. It seeks not to surpass the self but to extend it, to keep it alive in one's children. Anyone who called this the most natural thing in the world would not be wrong, but this very fact leads to the crucial source of discord that vexes and rends the love between parent and child. If the child is an extension of the self, where does the parent end and the child begin?

The desire to extend oneself in one's children comes in other forms besides the purely biological. At the end of *The Selfish Gene*, Dawkins presents a concept for which he has created his own name: *memes*. This term, which has gained some currency in the decades since Dawkins's book appeared, refers to what Dawkins calls "a unit of cultural transmission." Memes can consist of patterns of thought, concepts, ideas, and much more. As examples, he cites "tunes, ideas, catch-phrases, clothes fashions, ways of making pots or building arches."[13] Einstein's equation $E = mc^2$ is a meme; so is knowing how to build a canoe. Parents impart these units of cultural transmission to their children along with their hair color and the shape of their noses. But these memes are not just matters of information or technological know-how; they also include deeply rooted stances toward life, which are often positive and just as often not so positive. It is these memes, just as much as their genetic material, that parents try to perpetuate in their children. They always succeed.

The Bible has it as a command: "Honor thy father and mother." There may be a sense in which it is not an imperative but a statement of fact. You *will* honor your father and mother, whether you want to or not.

This idea forms the core insight of one of the twentieth century's most improbable psychological innovators, Bob Hoffman (1921–1997). Originally a tailor in Oakland, California, at some point in his life Hoffman discovered that he had paranormal powers and began to work as a psychic consultant. Even this unusual career path took another sudden bend when Hoffman believed he was contacted by a deceased friend, a Dr. Siegfried Fischer, who taught him a process of personal transformation that Fischer had learned on the other side of the gates of death. One night Fischer took Hoffman through this process on the astral plane (an alternate reality that includes the world of dreams), involving what Hoffman would later call "getting a loving divorce from Mom and Dad."

In 1967 Hoffman began to teach the Fischer-Hoffman Process, as he called it in tribute to his late friend and instructor.

In the 1970s, with the help of psychiatrists Claudio Naranjo and Ernest Pecci, Hoffman turned it into a structured and intense thirteen-week course and founded the Hoffman Quadrinity Institute to promote it. Later he dropped Fischer's name at the request of Fischer's family.

Hoffman was not an easy man to deal with, and he went through several schisms with his colleagues. Pecci left him to teach his own version of the process, and another group of therapists at the Hoffman Quadrinity Institute broke with Hoffman in 1984 to found the Pacific Process Institute, now known as the Institute for Personal Change. In 1985 Hoffman revised his curriculum to fit into an eight-day residential workshop and reconstructed his organization, now called the Hoffman Institute, which still continues to teach the method. Hoffman retired from teaching in 1991 and died in 1997.

The Hoffman Process (its current name) has won accolades from many leaders in the New Age and human-potential communities. Its alumni include the former astronaut Edgar Mitchell, the author John Bradshaw, the psychologist Joan Borysenko, and Ken Blanchard, author of *The One Minute Manager* and *Lead Like Jesus*. The process is centered around one insight: the concept of *negative love*. According to Hoffman, a human being acquires all negative traits from his or her parents in a subtle but easily understandable way. The child, feeling deprived of love from its parents (as nearly all children do at some point or another), decides to imitate the parents' negative traits in the hope that they will love it. The fact that this process is almost entirely unconscious makes it all the more powerful.

I took the Hoffman Quadrinity Process in the fall of 1982, when it was still nonresidential and lasted thirteen weeks. They were the most intense thirteen weeks I have ever spent. Several evenings each week I would make my way down to a deserted and unsafe industrial neighborhood in the southeastern corner of San Francisco, where, in a featureless classroom along with about thirty others, I would listen to lectures about the negative influence of our parents and the way to free ourselves from it. We were to take notes on our experience during the lectures, write them up, and turn them in to our own individual counselors. As additional homework, we had to search the inventories of our minds and find memories of negative experiences with each parent in turn. We were also to make a scrupulous examination of our own faults. Eventually, we would connect them with the negative experiences we could remember.

If this sounds like an enormous amount of work, it was. By the time I was finished with the process, I had amassed over six hundred typed pages of notes, recollections, and responses to exercises. In addition, each of us had to make a chart of our negative traits on large sheets of butcher paper that then had to be taped together. When mine was done, it looked like an Amazon of negative traits, with tributaries and subtributaries, and more than covered the living room floor of my apartment.

All this inventory was merely preliminary. The crucial act—and this had to be done twice, once for each parent—was to smash the inner images of one's parents by repeatedly walloping a large, stiff, specially made pillow with a Wiffle ball bat. There was a point at which we were supposed to "break through," a moment when the anger against mother and father turned into victory, triumph, and ecstasy. As subjective as this might sound, it was obvious to students and instructors alike when this point had been reached. I was among the slowest in the class. Weighed down by an oppressive fatigue that I knew was my own resistance, I took longer even than the many hours allotted for the practice and had to go off and spend extra time working on my own. But somehow I managed to do it.

The "quadrinity" of which Hoffman speaks is the human entity divided into four parts: body, emotions, intellect, and the spiritual self. By Hoffman's theory, the emotions, damaged by trauma in the early years, remain at a childlike level, imitating the parents' negative patterns in the unconscious hope that this will somehow enable the individual to be loved. "Breaking through" frees the emotional child from this bondage. Guided meditations were used to help the child grow into an emotional adult and to adopt the spiritual self as a more loving and genuine inner parent.

For all its merciless indictments, the Hoffman Process is not meant to alienate children from their parents. After the participant has broken through, he goes through another inventory of memories, this time focusing on positive experiences with the parents. Then he visualizes the *parent's* childhood as accurately as possible, with all the traumas and pain that this involved. Participants often realize that their parents' childhoods were far worse than their own. Finally, the individual goes through a process of forgiving the parents so that the chain of negative love that has spanned the generations may finally be broken.

From my own experience a quarter century ago, I could not recommend the Hoffman Process unequivocally. The process as a whole reminded me of a contractor who goes through a house knocking down walls without bothering to find out whether they are load-bearing or not. It's not always easy in practice to select out the negative traits alone for destruction. Certain necessary psychic structures that have been created by the parents may be destroyed as well, and they are not easily repaired. It is possible that the process has been refined in the years since I went through it and has eliminated these problems.

Despite these reservations, I have never doubted that Hoffman was right in saying that the evil in the human soul is transmitted chiefly through negative love. This, I believe, is the true meaning of original sin. It is not a hereditary divine curse or a stain on the soul handed down from Adam; it is the harmful patterns that parents, having received them from their own parents, pass on to their children. Sometimes the parent is victimized in the world and takes it out on his family at home. One of the most haunting expressions of this idea appears in James Joyce's story "Counterparts." The chief character, a minor clerk named Farrington, suffers a series of humiliations at work and at the pub. "He had done for himself in the office, pawned his watch, spent all his money; and he had not even got drunk." Going home, he finds his house dark and cold. Blaming his small son for letting the stove go out, he begins to wallop the boy with his walking stick. The story ends with the boy squealing, "I'll say a *Hail Mary* for you, pa, if you don't beat me. . . . I'll say a *Hail Mary*. . . ."[14]

Joyce goes no further, but psychology tells us what is to come. The boy grows up to be an abusive father to a son that is abusive in his turn, thus perpetuating the cycle of evil through the centuries. While certain feminists may blame men for most or all of this evil, I see no evidence that mothers on the whole behave any better. The God of the Old Testament says, "I the Lord thy God am a jealous God, visiting the iniquity of the fathers upon the children unto the third and fourth generation of them that hate me" (Exodus 20:5). If there is any truth to this threat, Bob Hoffman's negative love is the means by which it is accomplished.

Parents thus transmit a mixed bag of goods to their children, much of it unintentionally or even against their own best intentions. But the child often cannot permit itself—at least in its early years—to doubt its parents' love, because almost inevitably the parents have also bestowed upon it tremendous amounts of tenderness and care. Love and hate, terror and adoration are served up to us on the same platter. This alone goes far toward explaining our conflicts and ambivalences about love. If you can't trust your own parents, whom can you trust?

And yet abuse is abuse, and the child at some point comes to realize that what the parents called love is not what love really is. The consequences are often far more extreme than merely beating a pillow with a plastic bat. The literature of the world is full of stories about children who take vengeance on their parents. Greek tragedy could not have existed without these motifs. And for Freud, as is well known, ambivalence toward the parent (particularly the parent of the opposite sex) is one of the linchpins of neurosis.

Freud attributes this tension to the Oedipus complex. The child in its earliest years conceives a passion for the parent of the opposite sex, along with a feeling of rivalry toward the parent of the same sex. While Freud took the name from Sophocles' great tragedy, in which Oedipus finds that he has unwittingly killed his father and married his mother, the theme resounds in many other often unexpected places. One of the first descriptions of the Oedipus complex in world literature appears in the *Bardo Thödol*, better known as *The Tibetan Book of the Dead*. Tradition attributes this profound work to Guru Padmasambhava, the semilegendary magus who brought Buddhism to Tibet in the eighth century A.D. The book is designed to be read in the presence of a dying or newly dead person in order to liberate her from the cycle of birth and death. In a passage telling the deceased how to close the "womb entrance" so as to keep from reincarnating, the text says:

> If you are to be born as a male, you will experience the perceptions of a male. You will feel intense aversion towards the father and you will feel jealousy and attachment towards the mother. If you are to be born as a female, you will experience the perceptions of a female. You will feel intense envy and jealousy towards the mother and you will feel intense attachment and affection towards the father. This [emotional arousal] will cause you to enter a womb.[15]

What may be most remarkable about this passage is that it places the nexus of the Oedipus complex in a realm beyond the purely biological, before conception has even taken place. For the *Bardo Thôdol*, this unfortunate dynamic is the result of bad karma, the impetus of the individual's evil deeds from the past.

For Freud too, the Oedipus complex arises out of a kind of bad karma, although of a less metaphysical variety. In one of his strangest books, *Totem and Taboo*, published in 1913, Freud hypothetically reconstructs the beginning of the Oedipus complex at the dawn of human history. Freud half-jokingly called his account a kind of "just-so story," but he was committed enough to this idea to reiterate it fifteen years later in *Civilization and Its Discontents*.

Freud takes as his starting point Darwin's idea that the first human society was the "primal horde," essentially an extended family consisting of a dominant male, his harem of females, and their offspring. The females would be sexually off-limits to the male offspring, who would eventually have to leave to start "hordes" of their own.[16] At some point, however, the situation changed.

> One day the expelled brothers joined forces, slew and ate the father, and thus put an end to the father horde. Together they dared and accomplished what would have remained impossible for them singly. . . . Of course these cannibalistic savages ate their victim. The violent primal father had surely been the envied and feared model for each of the brothers. Now they accomplished their identification with him by devouring him and each acquired a part of his strength.[17]

This eating of the father inspired the sacrificial meal, in which the community kills and eats a totem animal (symbolizing the father) and thus both shares and ritually discharges the guilt. The pattern is echoed in the Eucharist, in which the body and blood of Jesus Christ are symbolically eaten by the priest and congregation. That Christ's death is linked to the participants' guilt is made clear in Christian theology. "He was wounded for our transgressions; he was bruised for our iniquities" (Isaiah 53:5).

The motif of killing one's parents, the father in particular, surfaces again and again in the myths of many nations. The Greek god Cronus kills his father, Uranus, only to be dethroned in turn by his own son, Zeus, and incarcerated in the hell known as

Tartarus. In the ancient Mesopotamian epic *Enuma Elish* ("When on High . . ."), the primordial gods, Apsu the father and Tiamat the mother, beget offspring, but the children's "hilarity in the Abode of Heaven" annoy the older gods, who resolve to kill them. Instead their grandson, the god Ea, kills Apsu. Ea and his wife Damkina beget Marduk, the god of order, who then slays Tiamat. Marduk's triumph over Tiamat, the personification of the victory of order over chaos, and his subsequent enthronement constitute the foundation myth of Babylon.[18] In these tales, theogony means parricide.

Given Freud's constant emphasis on the scientific nature of his theories and his equally relentless contempt for religion, it's curious to see his "just-so story" of the primal horde so closely parallel these ancient myths. Are all these stories the result, forgotten and yet unconsciously perpetuated through the mechanism of negative love, of some tragic conflict among our primitive ancestors tens of thousands of years ago? Freud thought so (*Totem and Taboo* ends pregnantly with the statement "In the beginning was the deed"), but we may also be dealing with an archetypal theme that presents itself both in the learned treatises of a Viennese physician and in clay tablets punched with cuneiform.

For a child to kill a parent is a monstrous act. Even in our age, which strives for novelty in its crimes as in its fashions, such a deed is a rarity. And yet in a sense the child does kill its parents. At the most basic level, a parent expends a tremendous amount of energy upon the child (sociobiologists call it "parental investment"). This is particularly true for the human race, in which the infant is unusually helpless for an unusually long time. Today the media occasionally produce estimates of how much it costs to raise a child. The figure is in the hundreds of thousands of dollars. While this may seem staggering, the cost is in a way less than it was in the past (and still is in many parts of the world), when it was not a matter of taking out loans for college but of deciding which of two starving people would get a crust of bread.

And this is apart from the childbearing process itself, which is excruciating and dangerous for the woman. ("In sorrow shalt thou bring forth children.") Some scientists have found that caring for offspring causes premature aging by creating DNA protein structures called "telomeres"—shortened strands of DNA that can no longer replicate themselves. One study found that women who cared for children with chronic illnesses had shorter telomeres than women with healthy children.[19] Although parenthood usually puts less stress on the father, many men have nevertheless worked themselves to death to feed their families.

Some parents resent this trade-off; most do not. They do not begrudge what they have given; they know it is in the course of things, and there are few parents who have not regarded the entire process as one of the most rewarding parts of their lives. But there is another sense too in which the child kills the parent. The child lives—is meant to live—after the parent dies. The very need for reproduction is the creature's acknowledgment of its own mortality. We are constantly told that life and death are counterparts, but we are rarely told why. This is why. The child is ultimately the only insurance the parent has against death.

Again we come to a perplexing impasse; again we face the dilemma of what is self and what is other. The child is *other* to the parent; it walks and talks and breathes on its own; but the matter is not so simple. The child is a continuation of the parent. To this degree it is *not* other, or rather it straddles the boundaries between self and other. One might also argue that the parent sees more of herself in a child than the child does in the parent. Hence the endless crises, which few families avoid entirely, over dependence and independence. The parent has extended—one might say extruded—herself into another being, but it is sometimes a torment to acknowledge the separateness of that being. The child has little conscious memory of the time when it was inseparable from the parent and so finds it easier to break the bonds. And anyway, that is in the course of nature. The child is supposed to move out and flourish independently, just as the males in Freud's primal horde were expected to leave and start hordes of their own.

In any case, it seems true that in family love, as in romantic love, the line between what is "I" and what is not "I" is not always clear. Efforts to clarify it may easily backfire. Often a son is never so much like his father as when he is rebelling against him. If the boundary becomes too blurry, however, one party or the other may have to shore it up. Everyone has to be weaned at some point or another, and a child who cannot leave the nest sometimes has to be pushed out. We are close to the members of our family, but an unerring impulse in us draws away when the closeness grows too great.

You may complain that I'm reading too much into things, that family life is simpler and more cheerful than that; it's more like a gathering of loved ones around a warm Thanksgiving dinner than an array of tragic heroes butchering their parents. No doubt this is often true from day to day. Nonetheless, when I think of family life even in its coziest aspects, I'm reminded of the Hobbits of the Shire at the outset of J.R.R. Tolkien's *Lord of the Rings*, who live in comfortable obliviousness while dark forces are massing all around them. So it may be even with the happiest of families. Unlike the Hobbits, however, the family as we know it faces the eruption of the dark forces of passion and hatred not from outside but from within themselves.

What, then, are we to do about all this? Are we to look at our closest and most intimate relations as nothing more than the clockwork of biology, the intricate calculations of selfish genes perpetuating themselves for reasons that they themselves do not understand? Up to a point, yes. We frequently sentimentalize love because we don't want to see it as it is. Yet there is a point when we *must* see it as it is. This is the "cold eye" that William Butler Yeats tells us to cast "on life, on death."[20] The danger lies not in taking this step but in stopping at this step. The cold eye has to be counterbalanced with a warm heart, with a love that can see the darkest and most mindless aspects of human nature unflinchingly and yet without cruelty or despair—a love that both sees all and forgives all. It is not an easy balance to keep. Too far in one direction, we become cruel; too far in the other, we are deluded. But if we do manage to strike this balance, we may be on the way to becoming whole. This could be why Christ urges us to be "wise as serpents, and harmless as doves" (Matthew 10:16).

All this having been said, the love of the selfish serpent can and does transform itself into conscious love. In practically every case, family love requires tremendous amounts of self-sacrifice. The Benedictine monk David Steindl-Rast has said:

> We always address the asceticism of the so-called ascetics, but very few people speak about the asceticism of daily life. At least from the perspective of a monk, the asceticism of family life is greater than that of a monastery. . . . Monks get up to pray during the night, but if they decide not to, they don't get up. There is no built-in absolute necessity to do so. But if your baby cries in the middle of the night, you have to get up; there's no maybe about it.[21]

The discipline is exact and rigorous; "there's no maybe about it." Everything depends on the attitude behind the discipline. If the parent gives the care because there is a sense of *my* child—if there is a hidden sense of property in it or, still worse, an attitude of grudging or grievance—the law of the serpent still holds strong. If, however, there is (and there often is) a sense of disinterested and unattached caring, a feeling that one loves not because the child is *my* child but because she is a being in her own right, with her own independent roots in the universal divine nature, the love of biology may have crossed over the barrier into the love that is truly free.

5

Making Brothers

Friendship dances around the world, calling us to awaken to the praise of happiness."[1] So wrote Epicurus (341–271 B.C.), one of the greatest philosophers of classical antiquity. For him, as for many of the Greeks, friendship sat at the center of human life.

Epicurus was a hedonist: he regarded pleasure as the supreme good. Today, when we hear the word Epicurean, we usually think of a gourmet or a glutton, but Epicurus' own philosophy was far more sophisticated than that. One might, for example, assume that a hedonist would be a sexual libertine, but Epicurus was not. He thought sexual gratification laid one open to far more suffering than enjoyment and was best avoided. His ideal was not immersion in the realm of the senses but what the Greeks called *ataraxia*, freedom from disturbance, whether from the annoyances of the outside world or from one's own baser impulses. He also thought that the pleasures of good company far exceed those of the carnal variety.

In 306 B.C. Epicurus set up his household on the outskirts of Athens in a location that would come to be known as the Garden. Here he moved with several of his closest friends, of both sexes, and here they devoted themselves to a life of pleasure. Although there were rumors of sensuality and excess, the life they lived was in fact relatively austere. Unlike his latter-day namesakes, Epicurus was satisfied with a simple meal of bread and vegetables and drank water rather than wine. "Send me a pot of cheese," he wrote to a friend, "so that I may have a feast whenever I like." For him, what one ate did not matter nearly so much as whom one ate it with. "Feeding without a friend is the life of a lion or a wolf," he wrote.[2]

While it's clear that Epicurus extolled friendship, it's not quite so clear why. It's true that the company of like-minded people is enjoyable in itself, but what happens when the needs of a friend go beyond the pleasure of companionship? If pleasure is the highest good, what are we to do when friendship calls, as it frequently does, for the sacrifice of one's pleasures, even if it's something as humdrum as giving up a weekend to help a friend move?

Epicurus' answers are ambiguous, partly because his views were modified by later generations of his followers and it isn't always obvious where his ideas leave off and theirs begin. In essence, he begins with rational self-interest. We seek out friends because of the advantages they bring, such as safety and comfort—things that clearly contribute to the pleasure of life. Eventually, however, a sense of fellow-feeling develops, and one reaches the point where one loves a friend as oneself. At this point one will of course be willing to make sacrifices on a friend's behalf. This is not, Epicurus stresses, as irrational as it seems—what kind of satisfaction can anyone get from a friendship out of which either party is prepared to flee at the earliest inconvenience? The very pleasure we take in friendship is rooted in the fact that we can rely on our friends. Even when we don't receive any immediate advantage from them, we gain satisfaction from the hope or expectation (the Greeks used the same word for both) of advantages to come. Besides, the sources of satisfaction are not always what they seem: we take more pleasure in conferring benefits than we do in receiving them.

In the end, these arguments sound like rationalizations, so Epicurus' views on friendship don't entirely add up. Friendship must be based on self-interest—the self-interest of pleasure—but if it is, it collapses on itself like a badly built house. Recognizing as much, Epicurus' critics in antiquity contrasted his own personal kindness and benevolence with the rather selfish philosophy that he espoused. For Epicurus the man, friendship was far more than mere barter; for Epicurus the philosopher, it may not have been.

Epicurus' views were shaped partly in response to those of Aristotle (384–322 B.C.), his older contemporary, whose discussion of friendship in books 8 and 9 of the *Nicomachean Ethics* is one of the most celebrated treatments of the subject. One of the central tenets of Aristotle's moral philosophy is that something you choose for its own sake is superior to something you choose for the sake of something else. Happiness, for example, is better than wealth, because we choose happiness for its own sake and wealth only for the things it can get us. (Whether this includes happiness is, as we know, a matter of long-standing debate.)

For these reasons, Aristotle regards friendship out of self-interest as inferior to one in which each loves the other for himself. In short, Aristotle is trying to distinguish between loving someone for his character and loving someone merely, say, for being amusing or pleasant. But is it really possible to make these distinctions in a cut-and-dried fashion? Maybe; maybe not. Where do a person's qualities end and the person himself begin? Epicurus tried to deal with this difficulty by saying that we love people for the pleasure they bring us, but as we've already seen, this approach has difficulties of its own. In either case we're left with an ambiguous dichotomy between the kind of friendship that is pure-minded, without thought of advantage, and the kind that has a very sharp eye out for its own advantage.

If the difficulties posed by friendship stymied Aristotle and Epicurus, it's not surprising that they often stymie the rest of us as well. Friendship is in many ways the purest and most disinterested form of love; it is more likely than romance and family love to be free from passionate and often insane attachments; and yet it can also be the most calculating and actuarial. We may (at least in theory) throw away everything for our lovers and kin, but with friends we are far more cautious. Christ says, "Greater love hath no man than this, that a man lay down his life for his friends" (John 15:12). Could this be the greatest love because it is the rarest?

Certainly we make sacrifices, often great ones, for our friends, but somehow the ledgers of debit and credit are never too far from our minds. In his recent book *Friendship: An Exposé*, Joseph Epstein writes, "A friend, a cliché definition has it, is someone who, when you are in crisis, you can call at 4 a.m. I'd say that's true, but with the qualification that one is permitted only one such call."[3] If you call a second time, your friend may still oblige, but with some ill grace; a third time, the favor will either be refused or granted, but in any event the friendship will probably be damaged. Unless, of course, the other party has had to ask an equally great favor in turn; in this case, the accounts are even and the relationship can continue as usual, just as you can rack up new charges on a credit card when the previous bills have been paid.

The accountancy involved here is subtle and, like the Equation, often no more than half-conscious, but it can surface in unusual places. We can see it in the most famous poetic celebration of long-standing friendship, the New Year's favorite "Auld Lang Syne," a traditional Scots song transcribed by Robert Burns. Usually only the first stanza is sung, but the last, though far less well known, is more revealing:

> And surely ye'll be your pint-stowp!
> And surely I'll be mine!
> And we'll tak a cup o' kindness yet,
> For auld lang syne.[4]

The lines "And surely ye'll be your pint-stowp! And surely I'll be mine!" don't make much sense in modern English, but they mean something like "And surely you'll pay for your own tankard, and I will pay for mine!"[5] The song, for all its praise of the timelessness of friendship, seems to be an elaborate prelude to an assurance that each man will buy his own drinks. Some may take this as evidence of nothing more than the proverbial stinginess of Scotsmen, but

I suspect that this kind of assurance undergirds most friendships. If one person pays for this round, the other pays for the next; if one person picks up the check tonight, the other one has to do it the next time. Only great ties of affection—or great disparities in wealth—may make it possible to transgress these rules, and usually not even then.

Similar rules apply to the most universal way of marking friendship: the giving of gifts. As beautiful as it is in essence, this custom, in our society and probably in most societies, is the subject of a dishonesty so profound that it almost amounts to dissociation. The official ideology, so to speak, is that gift giving is or should be utterly pure and disinterested, that "it's the thought that counts" and not the gift's monetary value. Etiquette demands that we take off the price tag before the gift is wrapped. If we find ourselves calculating the value of the gift given versus that of one received, it is with a certain amount of self-reproach. You're embarrassed to be caught making these calculations, even by yourself; you shouldn't do that sort of thing. But you do.

In an extremely influential article published in 1921, the anthropologist Bronislaw Malinowski explored economics as practiced by the Trobriand Islanders, a primitive tribe living off the coast of New Guinea. Some previous anthropologists had argued that primitive peoples were at a "pre-economic stage," having no economy. Malinowksi's field research among the islanders showed something quite different. It was true that there was no money as such. The closest equivalent was certain types of shells and ceremonial ax heads, none of which had any practical value and changed hands rarely. In fact, the islanders did have an economic system, but it was based on gift giving. Food and other necessities were distributed according to a complex system that, according to Malinowski, "enmeshes the whole community into a network of reciprocal obligations and dues, one constant flow of gift and counter-gift. . . . All their social life is accompanied by gift and counter-gift."[6] For the Trobrianders, gifts and commerce were indistinguishable.

Our own gift exchanges are just as commercial. Christmas, the great season of gift giving in our civilization, frequently becomes such torture partly because of this excruciatingly precise transactionality. The usual rule is that you have to buy a gift for everyone who has given you a gift last year or is likely to give you one this year. The delight of a surprise present is often ruined by the instantaneous realization that "I didn't get them anything!" You make a mental note, usually with a sigh of dismay, to repay the debt as soon as possible. At such times it can be a relief to run your mind over a list of friends and find someone to whom you don't owe anything.

By now it has become a part of the yearly Christmas tradition to denounce its exploitation by merchants and retailers—and justly so. But the commercialization runs deeper; it could not be exploited if it didn't. Christmas, like all other gift-giving occasions, involves as complex a series of transactions as Malinowski found among the islanders. There's nothing intrinsically wrong with this. The difficulty lies in our often obstinate refusal to admit that the process *is* transactional. We feel that somehow gift giving should be above all that, but somehow it never is.

Why? Why do we seem torn by twin impulses, one bearing us up toward freedom, the other chaining us to the ledger books? The simplest answer is that man is a dual being. He is, to use a phrase from one of the Hermetic texts of late antiquity, "a child of earth and starry heaven." The part that is of heaven pants for liberation from the dull echoes of reciprocity, but the part that belongs to earth realizes that things are not so simple. Materiality has limited resources; it cannot bestow favors with the abandon of infinity. It can do only so much, and that being the case, it must make its efforts count. Even altruism more often than not casts a sideways glance to its own interests.

A saying attributed to the Sarmoung Brotherhood, an enigmatic esoteric school from Central Asia, asserts, "There is no God but Reality. To seek him elsewhere is the action of the Fall." If there is truth to this utterance, it must encompass *all* realities, and if we are to be honest about our reality as humans—about what Martin Heidegger called our "thrownness"—we must acknowledge this dual aspect of ourselves. The almost unbearable tension between the part of us that is free and the part of us that is not is certain to stay with us to the grave. In the afterlife it may be different, but this is not the afterlife.

Something else too is at work here. If our transactions with our friends were entirely in hard currency—be it cash, Christmas presents, or cowrie shells—the situation would be reasonably clear. But the debts and payments are often in an entirely different type of coin. It goes under the names of affection, esteem, caring, and even love itself. This type of exchange leads us to the ceaseless calculation and recalculation of that most impossible of sums: whether or not we are *valued*.

We actually use the word, and its equivalents, in daily speech. How much does he *value* me as a friend? Is that all I'm *worth* to her? Don't I *count* for more than that to them? But how can we be appraised that way? The scales can never be accurate. There are no precise units of measure, and the reckonings vary wildly from person to person. What one individual means as an offhand courtesy is taken by the other as an act of deep affection (or vice versa). What is a mild joke to one is a mortifying insult to another. The financial section of the paper does not list the exchange rates for a kind word or a good deed. All of this opens us up to imagination in its worst forms.

The most trenchant examination of this situation that I know of comes, again, from Gurdjieff and his school. They have given this type of emotional accountancy the name *internal considering*. Gurdjieff says:

> On the most prevalent occasions a man is identified with
> what others think about him, how they treat him, what
> attitude they show towards him. He always thinks that

people do not value him enough, are not sufficiently polite and courteous. All this torments him, makes him think and suspect and lose an immense amount of energy on guesswork, on suppositions, develops in him a distrustful and hostile attitude towards people. How somebody looked at him, what somebody thought of him, what somebody said of him—all this acquires for him an immense significance.[7]

Readers may assess the truth of this passage by looking into their own minds, but again fiction affords any number of examples. In Wim Wenders's 1977 film *The American Friend*, a German frame maker named Jonathan Zimmermann (played by Bruno Ganz) is introduced at an auction to Tom Ripley (played by Dennis Hopper), a displaced American cowboy who deals in paintings of dubious authenticity. When they meet, Jonathan says to Ripley, "I've heard of you," and refuses to shake his hand. Ripley decides to entrap Jonathan into performing a contract murder, with disastrous results. Later, when the two have (against all expectations) become friends, Jonathan asks Ripley why he has done all this to him. Ripley says, "Remember that day we were introduced at the auction? You said, 'I've heard of you.' You said that in a very nasty way." "Was that all?" Jonathan asks. Ripley replies, "Isn't that enough?"

Gurdjieff's student Maurice Nicoll calls the narrative of internal considering "singing one's song." Nicoll writes:

> *"Singing Your Song"* . . . is based on making inner ac-
> counts—that is, feeling what you are owed and record-
> ing it in memory. Everyone has a song to sing in this
> respect. If you really want to know what kinds of inner
> accounts you have made throughout your life, begin
> to notice the typical "songs you sing." . . . Sometimes
> people sing their songs without any encouragement and
> sometimes, after a few glasses of wine, they begin to

sing openly. They sing about how badly they have been treated, about how they never had a real chance, about their past glories, about how no one understood their difficulties, about how they married wrongly, about how their parents did not understand them, about how nice they really are, about how they have been unappreciated, misunderstood, and so on, and all this means how everyone is to blame except themselves.[8]

So it goes. The mother complains that her children don't see all she has done for them; the children complain that the mother doesn't see all she has done *to* them. The artist who never paints a picture moans about how the world fails to see his genius. I have a cousin who was a major-league baseball player for a couple of seasons. At a family reunion he told me at great length how the team had mistreated him, the manager did not understand him — in short, how he had been wronged from start to finish. Somehow my aunt, who had organized the reunion, got a sports reporter from the local paper to come and interview him. The next day the paper ran an article that replicated almost to a word what my cousin had told me. But my cousin launched into a tirade about how the *reporter* had misunderstood him, had gotten nothing right, and so on.

At the same time as we're going through these mental contortions, we're putting ourselves through a parallel set of gymnastics to see if we're properly considering others. Much of social life consists of this kind of considering. Say a woman receives a dinner invitation from someone she dislikes. The thought of accepting fills her with immediate disgust, and if she were to suit herself, she would refuse. Instead she goes through all sorts of inner torture, imagining that she is bad and wrong for not liking the person who has invited her and that the only way she can prove that she is a good person is to accept, even though this is sure to produce an evening of misery for herself and quite likely for all concerned. The objective is, at all costs, to seem like a nice person, and a nice person does not refuse dinner invitations just because she feels like it. If she does refuse, she may torture herself about it for years to come. The same holds true for many breaches of social convention: not returning a phone call, an e-mail message, a card, a gift.

If the woman looks into her own mind, she will probably notice a curious interplay. Seeming like a nice person to others is the only way to make sure that she will seem like a nice person to herself. This is how the ego works. It has no firm ground to stand on (it is symbolized in Christ's parable by the house built on sand), and it must constantly keep its eye on others to gauge its value even in its own sight.

We might overhastily conclude that all this self-torture is the operation of conscience: self-reproach for a failure of moral duty. But there is a crucial difference between internal considering and true conscience. Internal considering has nothing like a genuinely accurate sense of moral valuation. A man may feel bitter remorse over failing to return one person's phone call while refusing to acknowledge that he has ruined another person's life.

This gross distortion of moral valuations is no accident. We may feel such guilt over our peccadilloes precisely in order to blind ourselves to our crimes. Frequently we are not only deceiving ourselves but taking enormous pains to do so. "We only confess to small faults to make it seem as if we do not have large ones," La Rochefoucauld observed. He also said, "There are hardly any faults that are not more pardonable than the means one uses to hide them."[9]

Where, then, is the remedy for internal considering? Gurdjieff also speaks of *external considering*. Here the focus shifts from self—particularly the ever-nagging question "How do I *seem?*"—to the other.

> External considering is . . . adaptation towards people, to their understanding, to their requirements. By considering externally a man does that which makes life easy for other people and for himself. External considering

requires a knowledge of men, an understanding of their tastes, habits, and prejudices. At the same time, external considering requires a great power over oneself, a great control over oneself.[10]

As Gurdjieff goes on to explain, this "great control" involves mastering one's own automatic reactions, including one's automatic reactions of helping. Very often attempts to "help" another person consist of nothing more than pointing out his faults, where he has gone wrong, why he is making a mess of his life. This is particularly common between parents and children. Sometimes it descends to absurd lengths. An old woman who can no longer even take care of herself nags her daughter about how she is doing everything wrong and botching her life. Of course, everyone knows what is best for the other, just as a man knows the solution for peace in the Middle East even though he can't get along with his family, or he knows the best way to fix the federal deficit but can't balance his checkbook.

External considering, by contrast, is in its true sense nothing more than an exotic name for putting oneself in another's shoes. It is expressed in the Golden Rule, although better, perhaps, by Bernard Shaw's version: "Do not do unto others as you would that they should do unto you. Their tastes may not be the same."[11]

Another version might be expressed as follows: *If you can do something kind, do it. If you can avoid doing something unkind, avoid it.* Kindness and its relatives—love, compassion, caring—are not always available to us. Nor am I speaking entirely of circumstantial or material obstacles. There are times when our own emotions make kindness impossible, when anger, frustration, or sheer exhaustion prevent us from doing what is decent or good. But these occasions are relatively rare. Far more frequent are the situations when kindness *is* possible, when hostility and insult *can* be avoided. It is, I would say, the mark of a reasonable and realistic morality to recognize such occasions and make the best use of them.

In any event, external considering is the art of gauging the other person's tastes and adapting oneself to them. And it is an art. It has rules and guidelines, but they can't be applied automatically, any more than one can automatically apply the dicta of an etiquette book or for that matter the teachings of the Gospels.

The most crucial characteristic of external considering is that it is free from *seeming*. It is genuinely concerned with the other; it does not do its good deeds with one eye in the mirror. Sometimes it may be indifferent to or contemptuous of how it may seem, just as Cordelia in the opening scene of *King Lear* spurns her father's demand for proof of her love, even though she is the only one of his daughters who really loves him.

An even more profound story is told in the Qur'an, where Moses meets with an unnamed "servant" of God—sometimes identified with Khidr, the mysterious hidden prophet of Islam—and asks to learn from him. The servant of God agrees, but only on the condition that Moses not ask him to explain anything he has done. Moses agrees. They begin to travel until they come to a boat. The servant of God makes a hole in the bottom of it. Moses asks him, "Hast thou made a hole in it to drown its occupants?" The servant of God refuses to reply. They proceed further and encounter a boy. The servant of God kills him. Moses says, "Hast thou slain an innocent person, not guilty of slaying another?" Again the servant of God refuses to explain.

Finally, the two come to a city whose inhabitants refuse to provide hospitality for them. "Then," says the text, "they found in it a wall which was on the point of falling, so he [the servant of God] put it into a right state." Moses tells him, "If thou hadst wished, thou couldst have taken a recompense for it."

At this point the servant of God tells Moses that they must part company because he has broken their agreement. But before taking his leave, the stranger explains what he has done. He made a hole in the boat to keep it from being seized by a king who was taking boats by force. He killed the boy because he was bad and his parents were good, and he did not want them to be infected by their son's evil. He repaired the city wall because it hid a treasure that belonged to two orphan boys that they were destined to find when they had grown. "This," says the servant of God, "is the significance of that with which thou couldst not have patience."[12]

Like any sacred text, this parable has many levels of meaning, most obviously the inscrutability of Providence. But the story also draws a contrast between Moses—the type of the lawgiver, that is, the upholder of conventional custom—and the unnamed servant of God, who is clearly a being at a higher level: he behaves with true kindness, which has nothing to do with *seeming* good. Few of us, of course, are in a position to see a situation with the clairvoyant insight of the servant of God. Even so, if we become able to act with some relative freedom from seeming, we begin to move from internal to external considering, and genuine kindness—and genuine friendship—begins to take root.

As friendship progresses, it evolves in another way as well. Most genuine friendships begin with either a similarity or a complementarity of character. The two of you may be radically alike or different in such a way that each compensates for the other, like Don Quixote and Sancho Panza. In either case your friend seems to "get" you, sometimes immediately. Such an experience is described by the sixteenth-century French philosopher Michel de Montaigne as he recalls his meeting with his closest friend, Étienne de la Boétie:

> We were seeking each other before we set eyes on each other because of the reports we had heard . . . We embraced each other by our names. And at our first meeting, which chanced to be at a great crowded town festival, we found ourselves so taken with each other, so well acquainted, so bound together, that from that time on nothing was so close to us as each other.[13]

Montaigne's friendship with de la Boétie lasted for the rest of the latter's life (he died four years after their meeting). It does not always turn out this way. Even when you feel an instant affinity for someone, what you took to be understanding may have been a more or less accidental similarity of responses. Seeing things the same way as another person is the seed of empathy, so to speak, but it is not empathy itself. As with marriage, the test comes in the living of the relationship. Some of this involves sheer habituation, time spent in each other's company. A proverb says, "A man must eat a peck of salt with his friend before he knows him." Still, there is more to friendship than mere hours logged in together. Inevitably, small grudges and grievances, the detritus of human interactions, begin to accumulate. If these are not cleared up, they will eventually kill the relationship; people often cherish their grievances more than their friends. Only external considering—friendship in its conscious aspect, the capacity for genuine empathy, as well as forgiveness—makes it possible to clear away these grudges. Otherwise they tend to hide in the twilight of half-consciousness and lead, sooner or later, to a break.

Real friendship requires awareness—both of a friend's needs and wants and tastes and of one's own idiosyncrasies. Our opinions and prejudices form a filthy lens through which we peer out at the world. We may never be able to clean this lens perfectly, but if we are aware of its distortions, we may be able to compensate for them somewhat. This is best done with a light touch and a sense of humor. Many spiritual teachers urge us to smash or destroy the ego, but this approach often turns out to be futile if not actually harmful. The ego has a way of appropriating such laudable efforts and making them its own (this is traditionally called the sin of pride). Usually, the best way to free oneself from the ego, in friendship as in any other arena, is simply to see oneself as a comical character in a cast of comical characters that includes the entire human race. This liberates one not only from vanity but also from any sense of grandiosity that may accrue from one's liberation, real or imagined.

Many philosophers, in fact, have seen friendship in its higher aspects as a way of surpassing or extending the self ("a friend is another self," said an ancient Greek proverb).[14] Montaigne wrote, "In the friendship which I am talking about, souls are mingled and confounded in so universal a blending that they efface the seam which joins them together so that they cannot be severed."[15] For Montaigne, friendship is a means of stepping past the stifling circumference of the self through union with another. Others have said similar things. The Russian Orthodox theologian Pavel Florensky (1882–1937) writes, *"Philia"*—friendship—"erases, if only in a preliminary and conditional way, the bonds of selfhood's separateness, which is aloneness. In a friend, in this other I of the loving one, one finds the source of hope in victory and the symbol of what is to come"—that is, in heaven.[16]

But this kind of self-transcendence is probably rare in friendship and may not always be desirable. Rather, I would suggest, just as romantic love attempts to transcend the self and family love attempts to perpetuate the self, friendship at its best makes it possible to relax the self. You sit and have a drink with a friend; you chat about things and people of interest; you even allow certain snippets of gossip to pass between you that you might not share with others—relaxing the self also loosens the girdle of morality. The joy of friendship, it has always seemed to me, is that it frees one from the labor either of perpetuating or overcoming one's identity. With a friend, as people so often say, you can simply be yourself. The ardor of a Montaigne or a Florensky in extolling the transcendental sublimity of friendship sounds a bit overblown.

On the other hand, my perspective may be unduly limited by cultural circumstances. This book is written in America, a nation that still in many ways imitates its mother country, and although we as nation are not known for replicating its *sang-froid*, traces of the cool British temperament can still be found among us. A Russian émigré friend of mine observes regarding hospitality, "In America one must be very careful displaying too much friendliness because it could easily embarrass the guest." This is particularly the case with friendship among males. It would be very hard for most American men to proclaim the kind of affection for a friend that we find in Montaigne or Florensky or for that matter in King David, who in his eulogy to his friend Jonathan (ironically, the son of David's enemy, King Saul; the enemy, too, is another self) wrote, "My brother Jonathan, very pleasant hast thou been unto me: thy love to me was wonderful, passing the love of women" (2 Samuel 1:26). A heterosexual American man of our era would balk at such a proclamation. Homophobia hangs over us too heavily; any such expression of affection between members of the same sex is immediately suspected of having an erotic component. We see this attitude in Richard F. Gustafson's introduction to Florensky's magnum opus, *The Pillar and Ground of the Truth*:

> Florensky's notion of friendship has a decided homo-
> philic, if not homoerotic, tinge. All dyadic friendships
> in his discussion are same-sex unions. . . . Florensky
> decenters heterosexual marriage in this presentation
> of ecclesiality in order to privilege pairs of friends. He
> moves the discussion of Christian life away from the
> union of the flesh to the union of the spirit. Marriage
> is understood as a remnant from pagan life, now blessed
> by the church; friendship is inherently Christian. To
> my knowledge, Florensky's *The Pillar and Ground of the
> Truth* is the first Christian theology to place same-sex
> relationship at the center of its vision.[17]

The assumption underlying this passage comes, like so many of our current assumptions, from Freud: since all human energy is essentially sexual energy, all affection between men is to one degree or another "homoerotic." It's unlikely that Florensky, steeped as he was in Orthodox Christian theology, would have agreed. If anything, one suspects that for Florensky, "friendship is inherently

Christian" precisely because of its chastity. Certainly *eros* and *philia* overlap; the schematic divisions between the different types of love are imprecise and to some extent arbitrary. But in general, friendship is characterized by the absence of sexual feeling, as is illustrated by the endless popular debate about whether a man and a woman can be friends. Nietzsche's opinion is worth considering: "Women can form a friendship with a man very well; but to preserve it—to that end a slight physical antipathy will probably help." I find this quotation in Joseph Epstein's *Friendship*, followed by Epstein's comment: "This much, at least, can be said: once sex, not latent but actual, becomes an element in the relationship, something other than friendship is going on."[18]

There are countless pronouncements to the effect that *eros* and *philia* don't mix, but there are far fewer explanations of why. The truth may be relatively simple: friendship is not subject to the Equation. You can relax with a friend precisely because you are spared the Byzantine chess match of the sexual game. Once attraction begins, the Equation comes into play, which explains why Nietzsche felt that a certain amount of physical repulsion would serve as good insurance for a friendship between a man and a woman.

Similar dynamics seem to operate among homosexuals. A gay friend of mine tells me that in the homosexual world, you can generally assume that if two men know each other, they have slept together. No doubt this is an exaggeration, but in any case there seems to be the assumption that the relationship will continue (if it does continue) by diverging into one of the two standard directions: romance or friendship. There are certainly, among both gays and straights, some relationships that manage to combine friendship with the occasional bout of sex, but this type of relation is, to all appearances, comparatively rare. "Friendship is beyond gender," observes Christopher Bamford, a contemporary writer on esoteric Christianity (and a friend of mine).[19] For the most part it is beyond sexuality as well.

For Florensky, friendship is elevated to the realm of the sacred. He describes at some length a little-known Orthodox ritual called *adelphopoiesis* ("making brothers"), a kind of sacramental blessing of a friendship. Although there are different versions of this rite, in general it follows this outline: The two "brothers" stand in front of the altar, the older on the right, the younger on the left. Before them is a lectern on which the cross and the Bible are placed. Prayers and litanies are recited to the effect that the two will be united in love. They are bound with a single belt, they place their hands on the Bible, and each is given a candle. Two passages of the New Testament on love are read (1 Corinthians 12:27–13:8 and John 17:18–26), followed by more prayers and litanies. The brothers then partake of the "presanctified gifts" (the bread and wine of the Eucharist before they are consecrated) from a common cup and are led around the lectern holding hands. A short liturgical chant is sung: "Lord, watch from above." Finally, they exchange kisses and the first verse of Psalm 133 is sung: "Behold, how good and how pleasant it is for brethren to dwell together in unity!"[20]

Viewing things in the light of today's concerns, some might see *adelphopoiesis* as a muted antecedent of gay marriage (and it has been invoked in this context), but this view doesn't seem accurate, since the Orthodox Church has, for better or worse, always denounced homosexuality. Rather *adelphopoiesis* probably is, as Florensky suggests, a way of combining *philia* and *agape*. "Just as agapic love must be accompanied by philic love, which is irreducible to but inseparable from agapic love, so liturgical offices of the agapic and philic unions, which are irreducible to each other, must coexist."[21]

It's necessary to pick through the theological jargon of this statement to make it somewhat clearer. For Florensky, pure *agape* has a chilly air about it. "In the common usage of the [Greek] verbs of love, *agapan* is the weakest and is close in meaning to such verbs as to value, to respect. And the greater the place that is occupied by the rational mind, the smaller will be the place occupied by feeling. Then, *agapan* can even mean to 'value rightly, not to overvalue.'"[22]

(*Agapan* is the infinitive form of the verb from which *agape* is derived.) I've often wondered how the New Testament would read if *agape* were translated as "respect." "Respect thy neighbor as thyself." "Respect one another, even as I have respected you." I believe it would be no further, and quite possibly closer, to the original meaning than the usual translations of "love" and "charity."

Because of this rather standoffish quality of *agape*, Florensky believes that *philia* must to some degree compensate. It must add a note of warmth and intimacy to a form of love that is, after all, impersonal. For Florensky, *agape* "does not include the idea of a spontaneous act coming directly from the heart, an act that would reveal an inner inclination." *Philia*, by contrast, is personal. The person is loved for himself or herself.

Early in this book I wrote that the standard Greek-English lexicon says that *agape* often connotes "regard rather than affection." So the lexicographers would seem to back up Florensky. Evidently, there is more of an impersonal quality to *agape* (it is extended to all beings impartially), but it would be possible to take this idea to a point where it becomes counterproductive and possibly dangerous. If we stress the impersonality of *agape* beyond a certain degree, it starts to feel like an internalized admonition. One loves only because one "should" love. This becomes an instance of the "law" rather than love as such.

In the next chapter I will try to show how *agape*, conscious love, can and must go beyond moral admonitions (including the admonitions of the Gospels) if it is to realize its full potential. But before I do, it would be helpful to look at one of the most revealing yet most overlooked contrasts between *philia* and *agape* in the New Testament. It appears at the end of the Gospel of John, and much of its point is lost because most versions use the word love to translate both *agape* and *philia*. Here it is in the King James Version, with the actual Greek verbs inserted in brackets:

> Jesus saith to Simon Peter, Simon, son of John, lovest [*agapas*] thou me more than these? He saith unto him,

Yea, Lord, thou knowest that I love [*philo*] thee. He saith unto him, Feed my lambs. He saith unto him again a second time, Simon, son of John, lovest [*agapas*] thou me? He said unto him, Yea, Lord thou knowest that I love [*philo*] thee. He saith unto him, Tend my sheep. He saith unto him the third time, Simon, son of John, lovest thou [*phileis*] me? Peter was grieved because he said unto him the third time, Lovest [*phileis*] thou me? And he said unto him, Lord, thou knowest all things, thou knowest that I love [*philo*] thee. Jesus said unto him, Feed my sheep [John 21:15–17].

Part of the point of this story is that Jesus is asking one question and Peter is answering another. It is almost like one of those stock situations in which a woman asks her boyfriend, "Do you love me?" and he answers, "You know I like you." But obviously, the passage in the Gospel of John is speaking to something far deeper. In the inner Christian tradition, Peter often represents much the same thing as Moses does in the Qur'an passage cited earlier. Peter is the guardian of the external aspects of the faith, the "rock" on which it is built. But there is only so far he can go (just as Moses cannot enter the Promised Land). The third time Christ asks whether Peter loves him, he must descend to Peter's level and use the word *philein*; only then can Peter respond appropriately. Peter can't even tell the difference between *philia* and *agape*; he thinks Christ has asked him the same question three times. So it is with external religion. Its task is, in large part, to uphold social codes and morality. Very often external religion is unable to go past the "love of the world," past the reciprocity that characterizes nearly all ordinary human relationships. Rather it is the "disciple whom Jesus loved," usually identified with John, who represents *agape*, both here and in much of the esoteric Christian tradition: the Greek phrase for "the disciple whom Jesus loved" (John 21:20) is *ten matheten hon egapa ho Iesous*, where *egapa* is a form of the verb *agapan*. Some esoteric

Christians have even said there is a secret "Church of John" that stands behind and apart from the external "Church of Peter."[23]

Discussing this passage, Maurice Nicoll interprets *agape* as "conscious love" and *philia*—strikingly—as "mechanical love."[24] For Nicoll, unlike Florensky, it is not that *agape* is cool and *philia* warm; rather *agape* is conscious and *philia* automatic. Nicoll is alluding to Gurdjieff's idea that man, in his ordinary state, is a machine, totally subject to external influences. If someone is nice to him, he is nice in return; if someone is nasty, he repays him with nastiness. It's almost impossible to avoid this kind of reaction entirely, but much of Christ's teaching aims at transforming such unthinking reciprocity. This of course requires tremendous discipline, of the sort mentioned in 2 Corinthians 10:5: "Casting down imaginations, and every high thing that exalteth itself against the knowledge of God, and bringing into captivity every thought to the obedience of Christ." It takes great inner mastery—"bringing into captivity every thought"—to love your enemies, to turn the other cheek, to go two miles with someone who has asked you to go one. Even to try to do these things demands willpower and conscious attention, as well as some ability to stand back from the habitual reactions with which we are normally identified. "For if ye love them which love you, what reward have ye? do not even the publicans the same? And if ye salute your brethren only, what do ye more than others? do not even the publicans so?" (Matthew 5:46–47).

The progression from the "love of the world"—*eros, storge, philia*—to *agape* is also a progression in awakening, even, we might say, in enlightenment. The "reward" of which Christ speaks would then not necessarily mean a reward in heaven. Rather it would be the creation of a real center in the core of one's being (known as the kingdom of heaven or, in the language of John's Gospel, "I am"). This center, this true "I" (as opposed to the ego, the false "I") cannot be shaken by external circumstances; it is the house built on rock. All of us have this center in embryo—which is why Christ so often likens the kingdom of heaven to a seed—but many fail to develop it. They are, in the language of one parable, like the seeds that fall by the wayside or are eaten up by birds (Matthew 13:3–9) or, in the language of another, like the man who builds his house on sand (Matthew 7:26–27).

Early Christianity had a term for making contact with the true "I." It is *gnosis*, which means "knowledge," but not knowledge of the conceptual kind. *Gnosis* is illumination, enlightenment; it is insight into the true nature of things, especially oneself. *Gnosis* was the goal of many schools of early Christians, who were for that reason called Gnostics.[25] Nevertheless, Paul reminds us that "knowledge [*gnosis*] puffeth up, but charity [*agape*] edifieth" (1 Corinthians 8:1). What is there in *agape* that takes us even past illumination?

6

The Cosmic Human

If there is a universal balm for the ills of the world, surely it would seem to be forgiveness. It ends all wrath, remedies all injustices, calms all sorrows. And yet, however widely praised it may be, forgiveness is not so widely practiced. Often when it is, it's felt as an obligation rather than as something free and natural.

Forgiveness is all the more difficult because it is an internal process. It's easy enough to tell whether you have kept the Ten Commandments—whether or not you have murdered, stolen, committed adultery, and so on—but exactly how do you know whether you've forgiven? The mind has an infinite number of nooks in which grievances can hide. You can easily think you have forgiven someone when some little irritation reminds you that you have done nothing of the sort. Much of the teaching of the Gospels has to do with avoiding hypocrisy—in Greek, "acting"; a *hypokrites* is literally an actor—but how are we to know when we've avoided hypocrisy in our forgiveness?

Much, in fact, of what passes for forgiveness is little more than a sanctimonious form of egotism. One "forgives" out of a sense of *noblesse oblige*—it is a condescension, a favor bestowed by a superior to an inferior. "The Song of Prayer," a booklet that is part of the *Course in Miracles* material, calls this "forgiveness-to-destroy":

> Forgiveness-to-destroy has many forms, being a weapon
> of the world of form. . . . First, there are the forms in

which a "better" person deigns to stoop to save a "baser" one from what he truly is. Forgiveness here rests on an attitude of gracious lordliness so far from love that arrogance could never be dislodged. Who can forgive and yet despise? And who can tell another he is steeped in sin, and yet perceive him as the Son of God? Who makes a slave to teach what freedom is? There is no union here, but only grief. This is not really mercy. This is death.

Another form, still very like the first if it is understood, does not appear in quite such blatant arrogance. The one who would forgive the other does not claim to be the better. Now he says instead that here is one whose sinfulness he shares, since both have been unworthy and deserve the retribution of the wrath of God. This can appear to be a humble thought, and may indeed induce a rivalry in sinfulness and guilt. It is not love for God's creation and the holiness that is His gift forever. Can His Son condemn himself and still remember Him?

Here the goal is to separate from God the Son He loves, and keep him from his Source. This goal is also sought by those who seek the role of martyr at another's hand. Here must the aim be clearly seen, for this may pass as meekness and as charity instead of cruelty. Is it not kind to be accepting of another's spite, and not respond except with silence and a gentle smile? Behold, how good are you who bear with patience and with saintliness the anger and the hurt another gives, and do not show the bitter pain you feel.[1]

Much of what the world calls forgiveness falls into one or another of these categories. The first form is a version of the vanity against which Christ so often inveighs: seeming like a good person in one's own eyes. It is the Pharisee congratulating himself:

"God, I thank thee that I am not as other men are, extortioners, unjust, adulterers, or even as this publican" (Luke 18:11). From this position of "gracious lordliness," a man bestows forgiveness as he might toss a coin at a beggar.

The second form is similar. Christ says, "Every one that exalteth himself shall be abased; and he that humbleth himself shall be exalted" (Luke 18:14), but he is speaking of humility in the deepest recesses of the heart. He does not, we may trust, mean the hypocritical humility that seeks to drag everyone else into its mire, moaning, "We are all to blame." This false self-abasement likes to quote the verse from Paul, "All have sinned, and come short of the glory of God" (Romans 3:23). So we may have—but whose agenda is it to constantly remind us of this? If it were a genuine call to humility, the one who uttered it might first apply it to himself and might then be silent. But as often expressed today—and nowhere so much as in religious discourse of all theological stripes—such declamations seek not to pardon sin but to reinforce it. This kind of false forgiveness, as the passage says, can even induce "a rivalry in sinfulness and guilt." People take as much pride in their vices as they do in their virtues—often more. The same is true of the third form of false forgiveness, the martyr complex, in which an individual holds up virtue as a mask for vanity. This is arrogance in the guise of self-denigration. It is the humility of Uriah Heep.

Having said all this, we find ourselves at an impasse. We know we're supposed to forgive, but we're not sure why. Mainstream Christianity lays it upon us as yet another commandment backed up by threats of punishment. If we do not forgive, God will not forgive us. "And when ye stand praying, forgive, if ye have ought against any: that your Father also which is in heaven may forgive you your trespasses. But if ye do not forgive, neither will your Father which is in heaven forgive your trespasses" (Mark 11:25–26). Whether Jesus really said this or not, it does not seem like an entirely satisfactory answer. God is love, we are told, but somehow his love turns out to have some rather substantial strings attached. A conventional theologian such as Reinhold Niebuhr might put it this way: "The mercy of God represents the ultimate freedom of God above His own law; but not the freedom to abrogate the law."[2] God is love, but the bill must be paid. God is love, but somehow one is still handed over to the judge and the officer, and one is cast into prison (Luke 12:58).

Whatever this is, it is not forgiveness. The whole point of forgiveness is that it goes past account keeping; as Paul convolutedly tries to explain in Romans, it cannot be reduced to terms of law and justice. Conventional Christianity has tried to address this problem with the doctrine of the vicarious atonement. Christ, the incarnate Son of God, came down to earth to offer himself up as a perfectly sinless sacrifice in order to blot out the sins of man before the Father's eyes. But why and how this should work is never quite explained; theology ends up having to invoke such things as "divine mystery" and "the inscrutability of God's will" to paper over the contradictions. We never quite learn why it is right and just that God should have gotten angry with the human race after someone ate a piece of fruit in Armenia six thousand years ago or why he should have had to send a part of himself down to earth to be tortured to death as a way of making it up to another part of himself. Put this way, it sounds ridiculous, but it is simply standard Christian dogma stated in plain language. Whatever meaning Christ's passion and death may have, it cannot be this. "God is not mocked," we read (Galatians 6:7). God *would* be mocked if this dogma were true.

Forgiveness, then, cannot be explained in terms of either justice or theology. And yet—and this is precisely where the power of the Christian message lies—it is still the case that we must forgive. Is it simply axiomatic, something we must take as a self-evident truth? Possibly, but there is another way of viewing the matter. I just quoted half of a verse from Galatians. Here is the other half: "Whatsoever a man soweth, that shall he also reap." This, in Paul's language, is what the spiritual traditions of India have called the doctrine of karma. The Greeks called it *nemesis*, or retribution. A given cause has a like effect; good begets good, and evil, evil. This *is* self-evident. We see it every day. If a man does evil to another, he is likely to get evil in return. If a woman does a kind deed, she will probably find that kindness paid back to her.

Taken in full, this idea is extremely sobering. "Use every man after his desert, and who shall 'scape whipping?" asks Hamlet.[3] We know we are not innocent. If the law of karma holds, then sooner or later retribution will find us. The philosophies of India have intricate explanations for why this recompense is not instantaneous: they speak of *samskaras*, which are in effect "seeds of karma" that will sooner or later blossom in the right circumstances, in this lifetime or another. Even apart from these theories, when we are aware of our guilt, we often feel that the hangman is waiting. This is said to be why some criminals, like Raskolnikov in *Crime and Punishment*, confess even when they have no chance of being caught.

Where, then, is the way out? It seems to be the unique contribution of Jesus Christ to find it in forgiveness. Certainly forgiveness had long been known and praised before the coming of Christ. Cicero, in his treatise on friendship, writes, "We must desire and wish that however often a friend might sin, he might have that many more handles that he might grasp" for reconciliation.[4] But it was Christ who elevated forgiveness to the core of human life. Why? By now it should be obvious. Forgiveness is the only way out of the hideous cycle of karma, portrayed in the Tarot deck as the Wheel of Fortune, a crude wooden contraption on which an ape and a dog are caught, with a rather stupid-looking sphinx perched on top holding a sword. So the Tarot of Marseilles, one of the more ancient versions, pictures this card. It doesn't take much imagination to see in it a resemblance to traditional Buddhist images of the Wheel of Life, which usually have a cock, a pig, and a snake, symbols of the Three Poisons of lust, anger, and obliviousness, placed in the center. But where Buddhism sees the remedy as cognitive awakening, Christianity tends to see it as forgiveness, which eliminates the *samskaras* of our own past actions to the extent that we ourselves forgive. If karma provides exact repercussions for our actions, then by necessity it would have to wipe out our offenses to the exact degree that we wipe out those of others. "Forgive us our debts as we have forgiven our debtors" (Matthew 6:12).[5]

Churchgoers will have long since noticed that this verse of the Lord's Prayer is recited in two different ways. Sometimes it is "Forgive us our debts," sometimes "Forgive us our trespasses." Which is right? As I mentioned in Chapter One, the Greek makes it extremely clear. The word is *opheilemata*, from the verb *opheilein*, "to owe." Christ uses the word "debts" rather than "sins" here. Why? Looking at the Gospels as a whole, we find that in fact Christ speaks quite often about money and debts. In one parable, a servant (literally, "slave") owes his master ten thousand talents—a staggering, almost inconceivable amount of money, equivalent to, say, a billion dollars today. The servant says he cannot pay, and the master forgives him. But the servant then turns around and has a "fellowservant" who owes him "an hundred pence" (or a hundred denarii, in any event a much smaller sum), cast into debtors' prison. The master then turns around and has the first servant cast into debtors' prison as well. "So likewise shall my heavenly Father do also unto you, if ye from your hearts forgive not every one his brother" (Matthew 18:23–35). To put it another way, the law of karma is inexorable. You will receive exactly what you mete out to others.

But what difference, really, does it makes whether we speak of debts or trespasses? The difference can be great. Those who emphasize the social aspect of Christ's teaching might say that substituting "trespasses" for "debts" was the work of a church that had become too intertwined with the rich and the powerful.[6] The rich do not want to be told to forget what they are owed. (One can only imagine making this statement to a conference of bankers.) The bonds of society are too intimately bound up with monetary obligation; suggesting that these should be undone, even to the slightest degree, is extremely threatening, especially to those with the most to lose. Changing the word to "trespasses" gets around this problem by limiting the scope of the verse to actual offenses. But this, I would say, limits it too much.

I am not proposing some radical social gospel or liberation theology that would put an end to economic structures as we know them. Such a thing might be possible in an ideal world, but we don't live in that ideal world. Socialists are fond of pointing to a verse in Acts that says, "And all that believed were together, and had all things in common" (Acts 2:44), but they are less eager to note that this idealistic form of communal life did not seem to last very long even among the Apostles and their students. And while the Law of Moses ordered that every fifty years there should be a jubilee year, in which "ye shall return every man unto his possession, and ye shall return every man unto his family" (Leviticus 25:10)—that is, debts were to be forgiven and slaves freed—I don't know of any evidence that this custom was much honored by the children of Israel in any period. Since human nature changes less than we often like to pretend, it's safe to assume that most people, particularly the rich, will continue to have no qualms about claiming their due.

Nevertheless, the command to forgive debts, not just "trespasses," still stands. How are we to understand it? The argument I've been making throughout this book should give some indication. We live in a world of reciprocity, of transactions. We incur any number of "debts" that are not really offenses or trespasses. We may owe someone a phone call or a letter or for that matter a greeting or a kind word. We don't always fulfill these obligations. The network of social exchange is so extensive that it's probably impossible to fulfill them all. But they sit at the backs of our minds, oppressing us and weighing us down, often without our conscious knowledge. Christ seems to be suggesting that we need not preoccupy ourselves with these obligations in a calculating or actuarial way, so long as we're able to grant the same favor to others. This is merely one of the ways in which "my yoke is easy, and my burden is light" (Matthew 11:30).

As comforting as this may sound, you may still be tempted to throw down this book and say, "All throughout, you've been indulging in a merciless indictment of the love of the world in all its forms. Nothing—sex, love, family, friendship—has escaped your cynical eye. Everything is one big transaction, a commercial exchange of one sort or another. And now you start to rhapsodize about forgiveness. Except it turns out that your so-called forgiveness is just as transactional as all the rest."

To such an accusation, I would have to plead guilty, at least if I were to leave the discussion here. Forgiveness may rescue us from the inexorable law of karma, but it doesn't seem to take us past transactionality. Money is still money in whatever form it takes, even if it is treasure laid up in heaven. So, then, is there no way out?

Not by any conventional understanding. Even forgiveness as the removal of karma is nothing more than an esoteric form of transactionality. If I forgive someone for not sending me a Christmas card, does that mean I should be acquitted of murder? If the answer is yes, it would seem to be a monstrous injustice. If the answer is no, then the laws of reciprocity still stand. Justice may be done, but justice is not love.

There is thus no real escape from the laws of the world in the world's own terms, whether we look at them from the perspective of biology, social obligation, family bonds, or even the comparatively esoteric considerations of the workings of karma. To understand forgiveness in its deepest aspect—and to answer the question left hanging at the end of the preceding chapter, namely, What is *agape* and why is it better than these other forms of love?—we need to look at reality through another dimension.

If there is one cliché that has been constantly drummed into our ears by countless religious leaders, it is the claim that "we are all one." We hear this so often that we take it no more seriously than we do a soft-drink commercial. And why *should* we take it seriously?

There is nothing in the world we see to indicate even remotely that it might be true. All over we see people jockeying for position, trying to surpass each other in money, status, comfort. One person's success means another's failure. At any given time, two different people cannot be elected president or win the Academy Award for best actress or be the richest person in the world. One man gets the girl, and the other does not. The verdict of appearances is obvious: we are *not* all one. Our name is Legion.

This is why, in order to understand the statement that we are all one and to see if it makes any sense whatsoever, we have to go past the evidence of the senses and the world we see. To do this, we need to look into ourselves and see what we are made of—not in terms of proteins and chemicals but of how we experience ourselves. Although I've discussed these ideas in earlier chapters, it seems necessary to elaborate on them slightly for my purposes here.

If you look into your own experience, you will soon see that it comes in two basic forms, one might almost say "flavors." There is the world of physical experience, of the outer world of the five senses, which is to a great degree public; we can discuss it and compare it with others. There is also the world of inner experience: thoughts, images, feelings, associations, dreams. This is more or less private (the dream I had last night is practically certain to be different from everyone else's). These two worlds have been given various names in different esoteric traditions. The Kabbalah calls the first world *Assiyah*, or "doing": the world of physical manifestation. The second is *Yetzirah*, or "formation": the world of images, forms, concepts. Esoteric Christianity refers to these as the body (or the "flesh") and the "soul" or "psyche," respectively. (The word in the Greek New Testament translated as "soul" is *psyche*.)

There, it would seem, we have the totality of experience: body and soul, inner and outer worlds. In fact, modern Christianity speaks of human beings as made up of body and soul. Ancient Christianity, however, said that we are composed of *three* entities:

body, soul, and spirit. "I pray God your whole spirit and soul and body be preserved blameless unto the coming of our Lord Jesus Christ" (1 Thessalonians 5:23). Soul and spirit are two different things: "For the word of God is quick, and powerful, and sharper than any two-edged sword, piercing even to the dividing asunder of soul and spirit" (Hebrews 4:12). What's the difference between the two? If you consult even the most learned authorities in contemporary theology, you'll probably conclude that they don't know. This is a crucial distinction that has been lost in Christianity, and Christianity has never been right since.

To go back to our own experience, we can see that although experience can be comparatively easily divided between inner and outer, between soul and body, what is left out is *that which experiences*. If there is an "I" that can witness even its own most private thoughts and desires from a remove, this "I" must be distinct from them. This is a very subtle but very profound point. It's not terribly difficult to grasp (although it will probably be easiest for those with a certain amount of meditative experience), but it is often forgotten. This witness is always *that which sees*, so of course it can never be seen. "What you are looking for is what is looking," said Francis of Assisi. The Hindu Upanishads say, "You could not see the seer of seeing. You could not hear the hearer of hearing. You could not think the thinker of thinking. You could not understand the understander of understanding."[7] Hindu philosophy identifies this witness with the *Atman*, usually translated as "Self." As I said in Chapter Four, the Gospels refer to it as "the spirit," "the kingdom of heaven," the "kingdom of God," and "I am." Some esoteric Christian texts, especially those in the Eastern Orthodox tradition, call it the *nous* or "consciousness." If one grasps this point, suddenly an extraordinary amount of what was baffling and cryptic in mystical literature of all types becomes remarkably clear.

This consciousness is not limited to humans or even to living beings but subsists in everything, no matter how apparently inanimate. Thomas Edison once said, "I do not believe that matter is inert, acted upon by an outside force. To me it seems that every atom is possessed by a certain amount of primitive intelligence. Look at the thousand of ways in which atoms of hydrogen combine with those of other elements, forming the most diverse substances. Do you mean to say that they do this without intelligence?"[8] Sir William Crookes, a renowned British physicist of the late nineteenth century, said, "Every atom has sensation and power of movement."[9] This does not mean that a hydrogen atom has a conscious ego like ours or even of the sort that we observe in the most primitive life forms. But under certain circumstances, the atom "knows" how to recognize an oxygen atom and "knows" how to react with it to produce certain chemical combinations such as water. From our perspective, this is mind at a very rudimentary level, but it is mind nonetheless.

We can take the matter a step further and say that this universal, all-pervasive mind is God in his immanent aspect: "For in him we live, and move, and have our being," as Paul told the philosophically sophisticated Athenians (Acts 17:28). Esoterically, this immanent aspect of God is called the "Son."[10] The Jews of the first century A.D., influenced by Hellenistic philosophy, called it the Logos, usually translated as "Word" but meaning something more like "reason" or even "mind"—particularly mind in its structuring and organizing aspect.[11] Because it's also known as "I am," Christ, speaking in the person of this Logos, can say in the Gospel of Thomas, "Split the wood and I am there": what in us says "I am" is also present in everything.[12] Christ, again speaking in the person of the Logos, also says, "I am the way, the truth, and the life: no man cometh to the Father, but by me" (John 14:6). This "I am" is the gateway to universal consciousness and beyond it to the experience of the transcendental Father who is the ground of all being. Such an interpretation transforms this verse from a narrow sectarian claim into a profound insight into metaphysical reality. The Greek philosopher Heraclitus said, "If you have heard [and understood] not me but the Logos, it is wise to agree that all things are one."[13]

Heraclitus also said, "The Logos is common to all, but most people live as if they had minds of their own."[14] Although the Logos, mind, subsists in all things, in day-to-day experience the "I" can be, and usually is, fixed in a stance of opposition against the rest of the world. It is frozen in egotism and isolation. Vladimir Solovyov observes:

> This abnormal attitude toward everything else—this exclusive self-assertion, or egoism, all-powerful in our practical life even though we deny it in theory, this opposition of the self to all other selves and the practical negation of the other selves—constitutes the radical *evil* of our nature. It is characteristic of everything that lives, since every natural entity, every beast, insect, and blade of grass, separates itself in its own peculiar being from everything else and strives to be everything for itself, swallowing up or repelling what is other (whence arises external, material being). Therefore, evil is a property common to all of nature.[15]

As Solovyov stresses, "radical evil" is not limited to humans. It is a universal force, which far outstrips the petty sins of a single species on earth. This is why Paul can say that "the whole creation groaneth and travaileth in pain until now" (Romans 8:22). We do not, probably cannot, know how this drama plays out in the lives of different species, on this planet and possibly on others, or in the dynamics of the universe itself. The twentieth-century French alchemist Henri Coton-Alvart daringly suggests that matter itself is constituted of the resistance of this radical evil to the light of God: "The regions whose extent is of the order of magnitude that we attribute to the atom or the neutron, or even smaller, are . . . *places void of light*, in which nothingness, the spirit of negation, exclusively prevails."[16]

In any event, what Solovyov calls "this abnormal attitude toward everything else" is not something that arose once in a primordial past. It occurs on a moment-to-moment basis. In humans it is largely perpetuated by the mind's own identification with its contents. There is a world of difference between having a thought and remembering that you and the thought are not the same thing. Most of what passes for waking life is in fact a kind of sleep, a half-conscious identification with thoughts and emotions, which inevitably imply a "me" and "mine" set off in opposition to the rest of the world. (The emotions in particular are, in the esoteric Christian tradition, usually called "passions," a significant choice of words in that it emphasizes the passivity of consciousness in regard to its own contents.) As many spiritual teachers have emphasized, it is necessary to detach the consciousness, the true "I," from its contents in order for liberation to occur. This is arguably what the text from Hebrews means when it speaks of the "cleaving asunder of soul and spirit." It does not refer to death but to liberation of the consciousness ("spirit") from enslavement to its own experience ("soul" or psyche). This is why practically all esoteric traditions put such emphasis on meditation, which is the day-to-day process that makes this liberation possible.

As the fixity of ordinary identification begins to dissolve, the psyche is increasingly experienced as a kind of flowing—the "stream of consciousness" made famous by twentieth-century literature. The "I" becomes able to watch its own experience as a film unfolding before it. But then questions arise: If all of what passes for "my" experience is in itself a sort of other—a film that I can watch from a distance—who or what is this mind that is doing the looking? And where is the dividing line between my mind and someone else's?

That is precisely the crux of the matter. As mind begins to dissolve its attachments to its "own" experience, it begins to regard itself not as an isolated thing but as part of a larger mind. There is no real border between this "I" and the collective "I" in which we all participate. This is sometimes known as "the I that is we."

Countless traditions from around the world speak of this truth. Because it runs so directly counter to what we usually regard as self-evident reality, these traditions have had to resort to myth or allegory to explain it. Often they start with what Christianity calls the Fall, the initial lapse of mind from its original state of purity and clarity. One example comes from the Zoroastrian religion of ancient Persia. It begins with the cosmic man, whose name is Gayomart. Ahriman, the force of death and dissolution, penetrates the body of this man, which then refracts into seven metals, as white light is refracted into so many colors through a prism. The archangel Spenta Armaiti collects the gold that is produced and nurtures it. Out of the gold grows a "plant": the first human couple, Mahryag-Mahryanagag, an androgyne, "two beings so like one another, so closely united with each other, that the male could not be distinguished from the female, much less isolated," in the words of Henry Corbin, the great scholar of Persian religion.

> However, since Ahriman had caused Death to enter into Gayomart, the structure of this total being . . . is unstable and fragile; it is not viable on the Earth, which is the prey of demonic powers. Finally, by the scission of its internal *dualitude*, this being gives birth to its posterity, historic humanity, the condition of which is the only one we can experience, and whose emergence is therefore subsequent to the great catastrophe, to the "day after," the invasion by "Evil."[17]

There is more in this profound myth than I can do justice to here, but several things are worth noting. Death, Evil, Ahriman do not mean physical death. Rather they refer to the force of egoism, the sense of "I" separate from the rest of the universe. The death of Gayomart signifies the loss of primordial consciousness through a rigidified sense of "I" and the subsequent birth of an apparent universe (symbolized by the seven metals) in which things, objects, and entities stand apart, seemingly existent in their own right, in opposition to one another. Even so, this sense of separateness is still relatively slight. It is only when the primordial man-woman, through the "dualitude" inherent in its nature, gives rise to historic humanity that our experience as we know it begins.

You will recognize affinities between this myth and many others, including the Fall of Adam (also a primordial man in whom male and female were initially united) and the myth in Plato's *Symposium* that tells of a time when human beings were androgynous and were only later split into masculine and feminine. At first glance these myths might seem to be simply trying to explain the origin of the sexes, but I would suggest that they go further. They reveal that initially, in this primordial state of consciousness, the distinction between self and other did not exist in the form that is familiar to us. The "male" and "female"—symbolically, self and other—were initially one; the "I" was still a "we." The division of these two through the forces of death and dissolution—a frozen sense of "other" or, to use the language of Genesis, "the knowledge of good and evil"—is the source of the world as we know it. The cosmic human was shattered into billions of tiny pieces. Each of us is one of those pieces.

Gnosticism approaches this issue from a different angle. The Gnostic systems are highly individualized; no two teachers had exactly the same one, and the second-century church father Irenaeus (one of our chief sources on the Gnostics) complained that "every day every one of them invents something new."[18] Nevertheless, practically all the Gnostics portray the cosmos as a series of emanations from a supreme, ultimately unknowable source. One of the lower emanations is a personage called the Demiurge (from a Greek word meaning "craftsman") or the Great Ruler. According to the second-century Gnostic teacher Basilides, the Demiurge is responsible for the creation of the universe as we know it, including the "Sons of God," fragments of the divine mind imprisoned in matter. The Demiurge also creates a series of subsidiary rulers or archons, cosmic figures that govern the realm of matter.

The Great Ruler, however, is ignorant: he fails to realize that there are higher levels of being above him. He begets a Son, who is wiser than his father and teaches him that he, the Ruler, is "not the God over all, but a generable deity" and that above him is "the Treasure of the ineffable and unnameable That beyond being and of the Sonship." And the Great Ruler "repented and feared on understanding in what ignorance he had been."[19]

This cosmology seems impossibly baroque, and we could easily toss it aside as a flight of fancy by some half-forgotten visionary. But if we view it as a portrait of our own cognitive experience, it is remarkably astute. The Great Ruler can be seen as a representation of the ego, which is extremely powerful: it can create a universe of its own, as in fact it does in generating our experience, individual and collective. This experience is conditioned above all by a frozen and diminished sense of "I," cut off from its connection to the universe and, in its blindness, imagining that it is supreme.

A Course in Miracles, too, stresses that it is the desire for separateness—which the Course explicitly calls the ego—that conditions our entire experience of reality, including time and space: "Time and space are one illusion, which takes different forms. If it has been projected beyond your mind you think of it as time. The nearer it is brought to where it is, the more you think of it in terms of space. There is a distance you would keep apart from one another, and this space you see as time because you still believe you are external to your brother."[20]

The Course is saying that time and space are merely arbitrary categories that we—or rather the ego, the Course's equivalent of the Demiurge—have imposed on reality. The farther we attempt to place it from ourselves, the more we tend to think of it in terms of time (because time past is irretrievable and time future unattainable). The closer we place it to ourselves, the more we tend to think of it in terms of space (because space, however remote, is still accessible to us, at least theoretically, *now*). But both of these categories are illusory, the result of the false belief that "you are external to your brother."

I'm using the term *categories* here deliberately to invoke the philosophy of Immanuel Kant, who defined the categories as structures that undergird our sense of ordinary reality. They include such primary things as quantity, negation, limitation, and causality.[21] As Kant emphasized, these are properties of mind, not of the thing in itself (the *Ding an sich*, in Kant's German): "*The understanding does not derive its laws . . . from, but prescribes them to, nature.*"[22] As a matter of fact, these categories block us to a direct and authentic experience of things as they are. Their equivalent in the Gnostic tradition is the archons, the "rulers" that keep us "each in his prison, thinking of the key," as T. S. Eliot put it.[23] By this interpretation, the archons are not evil archangels in the stratosphere but the very coordinates by which our minds structure reality.

Kant believed that these categories were absolute, that we as humans can never really go past them and directly experience reality as it is in itself. The Gnostic myths tell us otherwise. They are saying that these archons, these "rulers" of experience, can be transcended through gnosis. By this process the Great Ruler—the ego, which customarily acts as if it is supreme—can learn that it is part of a larger realm. This realization liberates the consciousness from the power of the archons, that is, from the constraints of time and space and causality. This helps explain why mystics frequently feel that they have been transported beyond the limits of the earth in their ecstasies. But since language is built precisely on such terms and categories, the reality that lies behind it can hardly be described, except perhaps in negative terms.

Such, of course, is not our day-to-day experience, which is all too easily cut up into conceptual categories. Esoteric Christianity depicts the broken shards of the androgynous primordial human, huddled in coats of flesh, in the figure of Adam. The Self or true "I," the part of the mind that is capable of transcending this isolation and restoring Adam to his pristine unity, is known as Christ. "For as in Adam all die, even so in Christ shall all be made alive" (1 Corinthians 15:22). This theme goes back to the earliest days of Christianity, for example, in the epistles of Paul: "So we, being many, are one body in Christ, and every one members one of another" (Romans 12:5). "There are diversities of operations, but it is the same God which worketh all in all. . . . For as the body is one, and hath many members, and all members of that body, being many, are one body: so also is Christ. . . . Now are they many members, yet but one body" (1 Corinthians 12:6, 12, 20).

Christ in this sense does not refer to the historical Jesus but to the great work of the restoration of this cosmic unity, in which each of us has a part, whether we know it or not. To quote Solovyov again:

> This body of Christ, which made its embryonic appear-
> ance in the form of the tiny community of the first
> Christians, is growing and developing little by little. At
> the end of time it will encompass all humankind and all
> nature in one universal divine-human organism, because
> the rest of nature is, in the words of the Apostle, awaiting
> with hope "the *manifestation* of the sons of God."[24]

Whatever connection we may make between this body of Christ and the historical Jesus, it is clear that the two cannot be equated in any simplistic sense. And while "the tiny community of the first Christians" may have also played a crucial role, it is hardly likely that they initiated the process, which in all likelihood has been going on since the beginning of time itself.

The theme is in fact older than Christianity. We have already looked at the Zoroastrian myth of Gayomart. The Hindu Rig Veda (dated from 1200 to 900 B.C. or sometimes earlier) describes the generation of the universe in very similar terms. The universe comes about through the sacrifice and dismemberment of Purusha, which is portrayed in the Vedas as Man, the cosmic human, but which—even more profoundly—means consciousness, "the seer of seeing," or as defined by the scholar of Indian religion Heinrich Zimmer, "the living entity behind and within all the metamorphoses of our life in bondage."[25] The Vedic hymn says:

> The Man has a thousand heads, a thousand eyes, a thousand feet. He pervaded the earth on all sides and extended beyond it as far as ten fingers.
>
> It is the Man who is all this, whatever has been and whatever is to be. He is the ruler of immortality. . . .
>
> Such is his greatness, and the Man is yet more than that. All creatures are a quarter of him; three quarters of him are what is immortal in heaven.[26]

What is most radically the Self, the "I," Purusha, is nothing other than this transcendent principle known as the Christ, an idea we also find in Paul: "I am crucified with Christ: nevertheless I live; yet not I, but Christ liveth in me" (Galatians 2:20). Indeed, Paul's entire theology is incomprehensible without reference to this truth. Without it, one might, for example, find oneself trapped in the endless controversy about whether one is saved by faith or by works. For Paul, it is neither faith nor works that saves us but union with this cosmic Christ by realizing that the "I" that lives is the Christ that "liveth in me." What it saves us *from* is not the banal hell of popular imagination but the true hell of isolation from the common life that pulses throughout the universe. In this light, we can see how Christianity may be rescued from the specious theological debates that have reduced it to a faith of scribes and Pharisees.

Although this long account of the cosmic human may seem like a pointless digression, it relates very closely to the subject of this book. The "love of the world," with its accounts, transactions, and agendas, is the love of Adam in his fallen state, in which each cell of his body imagines that it is, like the Demiurge, isolated and supreme and so finds itself fighting for position with so many other beings who deludedly believe the same thing. It is as if the cosmic Adam had been infected with an autoimmune disease.

Agape is the love of the cosmic Christ, in which each cell of Adam recognizes that it is joined to the larger whole, that what in it says "I" at the deepest level is identical to that which says "I" in everything else, human and nonhuman. Because this is the truth, to realize it is to achieve gnosis, to become conscious in the fullest sense. Hence "conscious love."

These ideas also take us to true forgiveness, to the forgiveness that is beyond account keeping. A *Course in Miracles* says, "All that I give is given to myself."[27] If ultimately there is no distinction between you and me—or perhaps better, between "you" and "I"—then forgiveness is the only appropriate response to another being. What separates us is ultimately illusory, as are all imagined hurts and offenses, no matter what their nature or apparent severity. "It is sin's unreality that makes forgiveness natural and wholly sane, a deep relief to those who offer it; a quiet blessing where it is received. It does not countenance illusions, but collects them lightly, with a little laugh, and gently lays them at the feet of truth. And there they disappear entirely."[28]

In one sense such a step is simple; in another sense it is not. The mind balks at hearing that so much of what it believes in is illusory. Illusory in what sense? Certainly the world feels real enough. The very word "reality" comes from the Latin *res*, or "thing." For us, particularly in the West, reality is inextricably bound to *thingness*—the thingness of objects, of creatures, even of oneself. The lines between self and other seem not only clear but rigid. Moreover, even if we grant in principle that we need to go past these lines, in practice it is not so easy. Going past the ego, the self as customarily understood, will probably feel like dissolution. And this the mind will not stand; its sense of self-preservation is far too strong. Whenever one strays too far past the boundaries of the self—through passion, through intoxication, through spiritual discipline—the mind will frequently recoil in panic. The Tibetan Buddhist teacher Chögyam Trungpa characterizes the primordial loss of consciousness—the descent from absolute knowledge into delusion—in precisely these terms:

> [This] consciousness arises when the energy which flashes out of the basic ground brings about a sort of blind effect, bewilderment. That bewilderment becomes... the basic ground for ego. . . . It is error that comes out of being bewildered—a kind of panic. If the energy were to go along with its own process of speed, there would be no panic. It is like driving a car fast; if you go along with the speed, you are able to maneuver accordingly. But if you suddenly panic with the thought that you have been going too fast without realizing it, you jam on the brakes and probably have an accident. Something suddenly freezes and brings the bewilderment of not knowing how to conduct the situation. Then actually the situation takes you over . . . the unexpected power of the projection comes back to you as your own doing, which creates extremely powerful and impressive bewilderment.[29]

This primordial panic, which precipitates the fall of consciousness into dualistic "reality," can be roughly equated with Gnostic myths of the birth of the Demiurge. In an often-quoted passage from the apocryphal Acts of John, the Demiurge cries, "I am God and there is no other beside me." The text comments, "He is ignorant of his strength, the place from which he had come."[30] The fallen consciousness, aware of itself as "I" but oblivious to its connection to the "I" that dwells in all things, cries out, "There is no other beside me." It is a cry of arrogance, but it is also a cry of terror.

Both Trungpa and the Acts of John speak of this primal panic viewed from the perspective of its descent, of the mind's apparent loss of contact with the common life of the universe. But it would be at least as useful to examine this panic from the other side, from the perspective of our familiar ordinary consciousness. If we attempt to transcend this consciousness, and if we manage to go far enough, we will come up against this primordial panic. We will then have to retreat or else go through it. Certain esoteric traditions call this the confrontation with the "Dweller on the Threshold." As is often stressed, it is a dangerous path, fraught with the risk of madness.[31] It is not unusual for someone at this state to be frozen in place, able neither to go past the Dweller nor to return to the comfortable oblivion of ordinary consciousness. Very likely this is a common cause of the breakdowns and "spiritual emergencies" that so many seekers experience at one point or another in their lives.

In the end, perhaps such confrontations are also misguided. Whom, after all, are we fighting with? With ourselves, as Luke Skywalker has to do in *The Empire Strikes Back*? This may appeal to a certain adolescent spirit of heroism, but it may be mistaken, and it also may not work. So too for many of the attempts of the spiritual teachers of the past generation to "flatten" or "destroy" or "smash" the ego (such violent terms are common). In all likelihood this approach will simply reinforce the primordial sense of panic that is the root of the problem to begin with.

Here is where we return to the main theme of this book. Love, as I wrote at the beginning, is what unites self and other. It does not attempt to destroy either self or other. This would be futile, for it is a radical fear of annihilation—Trungpa's panic—that has produced the ego to begin with. By contrast, it is love in the highest sense that enables one to relax the sense of self and other. The hard and fixed lines that cut the world into rigid compartments begin to melt and blur into boundaries that are far more flexible and permeable. If they are relaxed sufficiently, one begins to have a sense of the cosmic Christ, the great human of which we are all a part. This in turn enables one to relax these boundaries still further, until the distinction between "you" and "I," if not disappearing entirely, becomes far less vexatious.

Some of you may wonder whether this entire discussion is trying to trick you into dissolving into a faceless collectivity. This is particularly terrifying to Americans, who have enthroned individualism as a kind of pseudo-God. (The English say, "An Englishman's home is his castle." An American might say, "An American's self is his castle.") But if conscious love overcomes the false and tinny individualism that is represented by the Demiurge, it does not seek to destroy the individual as such. Here we reach yet another paradox. This relaxation of the self does not dissolve the individuality but transforms it, or, better, helps it become what it truly wants to be. That may be why so many spiritual teachings speak of "self-actualization" or "individuation." The "I" is not destroyed but instead fully realized, even though the situation may look quite the opposite at the outset. "For whosoever shall save his life shall lose it: and whosoever will lose his life for my sake shall find it" (Matthew 16:25).[32]

Indeed, the essence of Christianity is the elevation of the individual, not in the empty, vainglorious stance of the Demiurge, but in simple, human terms. This is one of the principal themes of Boris Pasternak's *Doctor Zhivago*, one of the most profoundly Christian works of the twentieth century. At one point Pasternak has one of his characters say, speaking of the Roman world:

> And then, into this tasteless heap of gold and marble, He came, light and clothed in an aura, emphatically human, deliberately provincial, Galilean, and at that moment gods and nations ceased to be and man came into being—man the carpenter, man the plowman, man the shepherd with his flock of sheep at sunset, man who does not sound in the least proud, man thankfully celebrated in all the cradle songs of mothers and in the picture galleries the world over.[33]

Conscious love is most emphatically not a wholesale rejection of the love of the world. The epigraph to the book you are reading is taken from an *agraphon* (uncollected saying) of Christ: "Be competent money-changers!" We can speak of transactional love as "money-changing." Christ is urging us to carry out these transactions well and honestly. There are "holy fools" the world over who have cast aside all social connections and obligations in an attempt to love everyone equally. Sometimes this is noble and beautiful and sometimes it is misguided, but it's not an example that most of us are likely to follow. We will still have our marriages and families and friends and even enemies. (Christ told us to love our enemies, but he did not forbid us to have them.) Those souls who can live on *agape* alone are probably as rare as those Catholic saints who are said to subsist by eating nothing but the consecrated Host.

Yet it's also true that Christ cast the money-changers out of the Temple. Whether or not he really did this in a historical sense, the symbolism of this act seems clear. There is a place for transactional love, for "money-changing," and there is a place for conscious love, symbolized by the Temple. But we are not to mistake our transactions for higher love. To confuse the two is to pollute both. This may seem an obvious point, but in practice it's not always so. Take, for example, the usual course of a romance. A woman falls in love with a man; she wishes him nothing but the highest good; she imagines sacrificing herself completely for his sake. But if the man should slight her, another side of her nature manifests. She suddenly wishes for multitudes of evil to descend on his head, and she realizes, if she cares to look, that her supposedly unconditional love was hedged around with any number of unseen conditions. (Men, of course, do exactly the same thing.)

Are we, then, to keep *agape* and transactionality separated in airtight containers? No. The entire thrust of this book is meant to suggest not that there is a rigid divide between *agape* and the love of the world and that the one must be renounced for the other (although many have made this mistake) but rather that each type of love contains a sort of gamut that runs from our basest impulses to our highest. In romantic love, there is the kind epitomized by the subtle manipulations of the Equation, as played out by pickup artists and the feminine wiles of *The Rules*; there is also the kind that, as Solovyov reminds us, sees an "absolute significance" in the other. Marital love can range from a type of bonding that hardly differs from the monogamy of birds or apes to the "conjugial love" that Swedenborg contends even thrives in heaven. A parent can love a child as a kind of possession, or he can see in her the transcendent face of a unique cell in the cosmic human. Friendship can consist of little more than an elaborate mutual exercise in internal considering, or it can express the kind of relationship that the Orthodox Church celebrates in *adelphopoesis*. Each of these forms of worldly love has its roots in the ordinary quid pro quo that is the essence of biological survival, but each also has a tip that extends to the higher dimensions, where it can breathe the air of absolute freedom and joy.

The Gospels urge us to allow conscious love to permeate ordinary love, to infuse our transactions with a broad and to some degree indiscriminate generosity. We are told to be competent money-changers, but we are also told to forgive others their debts and to give so that the left hand does not know what the right hand is doing (Matthew 6:3). (Traditionally the left hand is the side of judgment and severity, the right hand, the side of mercy and charity.) Many of Christ's most central teachings have to do with this issue:

> Ye have heard that it hath been said, An eye for an eye, and a tooth for a tooth:
>
> But I say unto you, That ye resist not evil: but whosoever shall smite thee on thy right cheek, turn to him the other also. And if any man will sue thee at the law, and take away thy coat, let him have thy cloke also.

And whosoever shall compel thee to go a mile, go
with him twain [Matthew 5:38–41].

Conscious love in this sense forms the main thread of nearly all
the ethical teachings in the Gospels, which in themselves constitute a set of techniques for practicing this love on a day-to-day
basis and enabling it to take root in the soul and spirit. The idea
of conscious love can be seen as the theory behind the practices,
not only rendering them understandable and reasonable but also
enabling us to feel them more deeply and carry them out more
faithfully.

7

The Special Function

In *World Light*, a novel by the renowned Icelandic author Halldór Laxness, two old friends, poets, find themselves in conversation. One, the novel's hero, Ólafur Kárason, is a ne'er-do-well, impoverished and abused. The other, Örn Úlfar, is a fiery socialist agitator, on the run from the powers that be. Örn Úlfar has taken refuge at his friend's miserable cottage, and they sit up all night at the bedside of Ólafur Kárason's dying daughter. As they do, they spell out the two great but opposing perspectives on human life.

Ólafur Kárason praises love. "Love, that's feeling for others—as I feel for my child when the waves of suffering break over her."

Örn Úlfar says:

> "I don't believe in love. . . . I don't know what love is. . . . Man has only one characteristic that equals the most commendable qualities of animals, one mark of nobility above the gods: he chooses justice. . . . What is love? If a loving person sees someone's eye being gouged out, he howls as if his own eye were being gouged out. On the other hand he isn't moved at all if he sees powerful liars utterly rob a whole people of their sight and thereby their good sense as well. . . . It is justice, not love, that will one day give life to the children of the future."[1]

The two soon part, Örn Úlfar to exile, Ólafur Kárason to a series of misadventures that finally leads to his suicide. But as this scene suggests, no sooner does the word love spring from our lips than we find ourselves asking about justice as well. If we grant that love is the central force in human life, how should we put it into practice on a large scale? Current society seems to rest on many foundations—fear, greed, wishful thinking—but love hardly seems to be very high on the list. Nor do I mean *agape*. If even ordinary transactional love were applied honestly and consistently in our society or in any other, most social problems would probably vanish as if by magic.

For me the awakening to these issues came in a rather unlikely way. It was the fall of 1988, and I had just left my job as an editor for a California agricultural magazine. In a hapless attempt at networking, I had invited an acquaintance of mine, an elderly gentleman who was well connected in the California establishment, to have lunch. Over a couple of glasses of chardonnay at an extremely agreeable seafood restaurant on the Berkeley marina, our conversation drifted to working conditions at the *San Francisco Chronicle*, to whose owners he was connected by marriage. I'd always thought he was somewhat conservative in his views, so I was surprised to hear him say, "If it weren't for the union, the employees wouldn't have any benefits. Because the owners do not care at all. *They do not care at all.*"

He said this with such vehemence that it took me aback. The owners of the paper were his in-laws, so I had to assume that he knew what he was talking about. Besides, I had just spent six years covering California agribusiness and had met many of its leaders. Looking back on my own experience, I had to admit that the overwhelming majority of them also *did not care at all.*

In the end, my acquaintance turned out to be utterly uninterested in helping me with my job search, but the moment of insight he gave me made that seem completely irrelevant (at least in the long run). On paper, of course, this revelation looks trivial.

Everyone "knows" that the powers that be operate the system for their own profit, that ordinary people are hardly taken into account, and that the poor are either ignored or exploited or both. These ideas saturate the newspapers and airwaves so thoroughly that we scarcely notice them anymore. But this kind of cheap, preprocessed cynicism has little to do with seeing the truth of the situation for oneself.

The issue of social justice has vexed Christianity for centuries. That Christ calls on his followers to help the poor has always been clear enough, even though the church, with its own unslakable thirst for donations, has often been more of a competitor than a benefactor to its charges. Indeed, mainstream Christianity has frequently shown a strange apathy toward the poor, apart from certain salient exceptions—for every Mother Teresa there have been dozens of fat and complacent prelates. The evangelical leader Jim Wallis recollects that when he was a seminarian, he and his fellow students decided to find out how much the Bible said about the poor. They discovered "*several thousand* verses . . . on the poor and God's response to injustice." Wallis adds:

> After we completed our study, we all sat in a circle to discuss how the subject had been treated in the various churches in which we had grown up. Astoundingly, but also tellingly, not one of us could remember even one sermon on the poor from the pulpit of our home churches. In the Bible, the poor were everywhere; yet the subject was not to be found in our churches.

One of the seminarians then took an old Bible and a pair of scissors and cut out any passage that made reference to the poor. What was left was "a Bible full of holes." Wallis continues:

> I began taking that damaged and fragile Bible out with me when I preached. I'd hold it up high above American

congregations and say, "Brothers and sisters, this *is* our American Bible; it is full of holes." Each one of us might as well take our Bibles, a pair of scissors, and begin cutting out all the Scriptures we pay no attention to, all the biblical texts that we just ignore.[2]

For this situation, we probably have to thank our Puritan heritage, which has always been zealous in condemning lust and sloth but has often elevated avarice to the status of a virtue. American Protestantism is so oblivious to the social aspect of the Gospels that its denominations are stratified by class, with the Episcopalians at the top and groups like the Assemblies of God and Jehovah's Witnesses at the bottom. (A friend of mine once quipped, "As an upwardly mobile Methodist, I've been an Episcopalian for years.") Today an individual's religious affiliation often tells far more about her status than about her beliefs. The sign on the church may say, "All are welcome," but to see one's decrepit Dodge in the parking lot next to late-model SUVs may give quite a different message.

It's also curious to see what constitutes charitable giving in the United States today. Many of its chief beneficiaries seem to be various self-aggrandizing foundations whose principal task is to provide steady income for their staffs and social prominence for their donors. Even when the money is ultimately destined for the poor—which is not always the case—the amount that actually reaches them is often extremely small. Some may leap automatically to the defense of such organizations, and it's true that many charitable organizations do a great deal of good work. On the other hand, as Ezra Pound wrote, "It is as difficult to get an American to think evil of a 'Foundation' as it wld. have been in 1860 to get a Russian peasant to spit on an ikon."[3]

The message of Christ is clear enough. We are to help the poor, and help them directly. It might be wise to remember this the next time one makes a charitable donation. But ever since Christianity became the state religion of the Roman Empire in the late fourth century, it has faced another dilemma as well: Should it try to change society so that these injustices no longer exist?

The question is closely connected to eschatology—that is, how we are supposed to view the "end of time," whose imminent arrival Christianity has been proclaiming from its earliest days. Many scholars have said that this was the heart of Jesus' own message. The greatest and most influential study in Christology is probably Albert Schweitzer's 1906 work *The Quest of the Historical Jesus*. Schweitzer argues that Jesus was an apocalyptic prophet who, believing that he was the Messiah and that his death would trigger the end of time, instigated his own execution. Since Schweitzer regards the Resurrection as a later accretion to the story, his Jesus is in the end a rather pathetic figure, and he sheepishly concludes, "We must be prepared to find that the historical knowledge of the personality and life of Jesus will not be a help, but perhaps even an offence to religion."[4]

Whether or not Schweitzer is right, it's undeniable that Christianity in its earliest stages was marked by a belief in an imminent Doomsday. This is the key point of the earliest New Testament text: Paul's First Epistle to the Thessalonians (dated to around A.D. 50). Here Paul is writing to assuage the fears of his pupils who are worried about the faithful who have died before the return of Christ: "I would not have you to be ignorant, brethren, concerning them which are asleep, that ye sorrow not, even as others which have no hope" (1 Thessalonians 4:13). Paul tells them "the dead in Christ shall rise first" and the living believers "shall be caught up together with them in the clouds" (4:16–17). This passage—incidentally the source of the Rapture doctrine beloved of today's fundamentalists—shows that many of the earliest Christians believed that the Master's return was so near that they were worried about those who died before it came.

This idea has been taken up again by each generation of Christians since then: the return of Christ is imminent. Why, then, should Christians bother about secular society? The New Testament scholar Raymond E. Brown summarizes this attitude: "Strong apocalypticism does not encourage long-range social planning. Structures in society that prevent the communication of the gospel must be neutralized. Yet precisely because Christ is coming back soon, other structures that do not represent gospel values can be allowed to stand provided that they can be bypassed to enable Christ's gospel to be preached. It will not be for long."[5] This may call to mind certain politicians today who believe that we need not bother about the environment or any other current problems because Christ will come back very soon and set it all right. Unfortunately, I suspect, we can't wait for the end of the world to solve our problems for us.

Brown makes his remarks in discussing Paul's Epistle to Philemon, which is written to a Christian in order to urge him to take back a runaway slave. What has struck many readers about this epistle is that Paul does not denounce slavery as an institution; he is simply asking Philemon to take back the slave as a personal matter. Slaveholders in the antebellum South often pointed to this text as proof that the Bible is not opposed to slavery. Of course they were right. Slavery was taken totally for granted in the ancient world, and practically no one—Christian or otherwise—called for its abolition or even seemed to imagine that such was possible. This may seem appalling to us, but it simply proves that the ethical standards of one age can never be applied exactly to another. It also shows that Christianity in its earliest times was not interested in changing society, even to imbue it with higher values.

What of more recent times? Pope Benedict XVI expresses a fairly typical attitude in his 2005 encyclical *Deus caritas est* ("God Is Love"):

> The Church cannot and must not take upon herself the political battle to bring about the most just society possible. She cannot and must not replace the State. Yet

at the same time she cannot and must not remain on the sidelines in the fight for justice. She has to play her part through rational argument and she has to reawaken the spiritual energy without which justice, which always demands sacrifice, cannot prevail and prosper. A just society must be the achievement of politics, not of the Church.[6]

This is reasonable as far as it goes. Few people today would want to have political and social life dictated by a church of any kind. And yet in the context of history, such statements sound disingenuous. If the church had always or even usually been an unambiguous advocate for justice and had shown more willingness to make some of the sacrifices that it constantly enjoins on others, it would be another matter. But the ecclesiastical powers have always tried to avoid such inconveniences. They have shown an ingrained preference for the status quo, for ingratiating themselves with rulers, however tyrannical, rather than standing up and awakening "spiritual energy" in themselves or in anyone else. The pope himself writes, "It must be admitted that the Church's leadership was slow to realize that the issue of the just structuring of society needed to be approached in a new way."[7] Even here, however, he is writing about the nineteenth century. The Roman Catholic Church has generally been far more ready to confess to its errors of the past than those of the present.

Often the church has used the secular authorities for its own purposes. The Roman Empire in its last phases might have done better to concentrate on fighting off barbarian incursions rather than ferreting out supposed heretics. And the Inquisition could never execute its victims directly: they had to be handed over to the secular powers for punishment. In exchange the church has frequently provided a validation, overt or implicit, of vested interests. In the early modern era, it was happy to endorse the divine right of kings but was far more lukewarm about promoting the rights of the common man. In the last century, it was eager to sign concordats with Hitler and Mussolini but reluctant to stand up and denounce their crimes.

The case of the Orthodox Church in Russia is even more embarrassing. Having been little more than a department of the state in the tsarist era, after the revolution it was co-opted by the communists, who promptly infiltrated its clergy with spies. It is estimated that in the Soviet period somewhere between 15 and 50 percent of the Orthodox clergy were KGB agents. One prelate even said, "I don't know what induced the KGB to make me archbishop of Vilnius."[8]

There is a kind of natural law that governs institutions: once they exist, their chief objective is their own survival; the purpose for which they were created has to take second place, when it's not lost altogether. This has proved as true for the Christian church as anything else. One of the most shocking things about the recent pedophilia scandals among Catholic priests is that when the hierarchy learned of these crimes, its first and greatest concern was to conceal them in order to protect itself.

Nevertheless, there has always been a small minority of Christians who have genuinely pressed for social change on behalf of the weak and oppressed. The Quakers' early agitation for the abolition of slavery, and their advocacy of humanitarian causes in the many years since, is one example. The Social Gospel movement in the late nineteenth century, which helped bring about the Age of Reform in American politics, is another. But many activists seem hopelessly naive. The liberation theologians of Latin America have accepted the tenets of Marxism more or less uncritically, even though Marxism has failed to create a just or even viable society in any place where it has been seriously tried. The peace movements of the past generation have seemed to operate on the entirely unwarranted assumption that if they cry, "Peace! Peace!" long enough, eventually someone will listen. The children of this world are often wiser than the children of the light.

I myself have no connection with any church or any political group, so I have no grandiose recommendations to make for any of these organizations. Those who feel committed to them will work through these issues as they will. For the rest of us, the question is thrown back to the individual: What can we do, or what can I do?

The two questions sound almost the same, but they are radically different. "What can we do?" is the cry of op-ed columnists and talking heads on television. It is provender for what one may call the "entertainment of conscience." Just as we go to horror movies to stimulate the flow of adrenaline with images of fright, we turn to the news to stimulate our compassion. The sufferings of the latest victims of storm or famine or war excite our pity, which in turn induces a kind of catharsis: having felt sorry for the victims, we feel as if we have done something for them. Such emotions serve as a kind of imagined atonement for our own relative comfort and safety, even and perhaps especially when the compassion is genuine. Nevertheless, the catharsis is rarely complete. Usually some measure of anxiety remains.

The truth is that it is impossible to help everyone. To ask what "we" can do is to ignore this fact. In an insidious way, it shifts the responsibility from oneself to an imagined collective, to government or society or the inevitable nameless "they," who, even if they were able to act consistently and effectively (as they rarely are), would still be unable to solve the aggregate of the world's problems. Deep down inside, we know this much. Gurdjieff gives this modern disease the name "vainly-to-grow-sincerely-indignant."[9] The indignation may be sincere, but it is also useless.

Trying to answer the question "What can I do?" seems even more discouraging. If governments can do little, what chance does the individual have? Apparently none. And yet this is the only way in which concrete contributions are at all possible. Individuals can and do make a difference—sometimes a crucial one. But they can do nothing with a scattershot approach. No one is going to solve the problem of peace in the Middle East while dealing with global warming while figuring out how to provide food for the world's starving millions. Even worrying about such things is usually a negative fantasy, the handiwork of the ego, which as usual is trying to prove to itself that it is a good person.

The answer, I believe, lies in a concept for which there is no word in English. In Sanskrit it is called *svadharma*, and it roughly means doing one's own duty. The classic text that discusses it is the Bhagavad-Gita, one of the greatest of the Hindu sacred scriptures, written probably between the fifth and second centuries B.C. This book forms a part of a much larger whole, the titanic epic known as the Mahabharata, which culminates in a great war between two rival clans, the virtuous Pandavas and the corrupt Kauravas. One of the greatest warriors among the Pandavas is Arjuna, and his charioteer is Krishna, the incarnation of the god Vishnu. As the lines are drawn up for the decisive battle, Arjuna sees his relatives and some of his closest friends on the opposing side. He knows that enormous numbers of them will be slain, and he loses heart. He turns to Krishna and says he does not want to fight; he has no appetite for the power or glory that victory would bring.

Most of the Bhagavad-Gita consists of Krishna's reply. It contains philosophy and cosmology as well as directions for yogic practice, but all of this centers on Krishna's urging Arjuna that he must fight. Arjuna is a Kshatriya, a member of the warrior caste, and it is his duty—his *dharma*—to take part in the battle. Krishna goes so far as to say, "Better one's own duty [to perform], though void of merit, than to do another's well: better to die within [the sphere of] one's own duty: perilous is the duty of other men."[10]

The word for "one's own duty" here is *svadharma*. It is not a moral duty in the ordinary sense: rather it is the duty that is embedded in one's deepest self. No one else can do the job that you were created to do, whatever it is. Liberation consists not of inaction or withdrawal from the world but of performing your duty selflessly and without attachment to results. Arjuna's *dharma* is to fight in this monumental battle, which has more than a political or even moral function. It is destined to bring an end to the age (much as the Greeks thought the Trojan War had ended the Heroic Age) and to restore a corrupt cosmic order.

The Bhagavad-Gita connects *svadharma* with the caste system, instituted by Krishna, the incarnate God. "The four-caste system did I generate," Krishna says.[11] The Rig Veda says that the castes were created from the different parts of the cosmic human: "His mouth became the Brahmin; his arms were made into the Warrior, his thighs the People, and from his feet the Servants were born."[12] This idea may horrify Westerners, violating our deep-seated ideal of egalitarianism, and it is true that India's caste system does not provide an example that other nations have cared to emulate. But we don't have to embrace the caste system either in principle or in practice to see an underlying truth behind it.

It's striking to see the same themes in the Western esoteric traditions as well. Swedenborg is the most anthropomorphic. He sees a specific and even somewhat rigid set of correspondences between the world above and the world below so that heaven itself is arranged in the form of a human body, which is the Lord's body.

> Since heaven in its entirety does reflect a single individual, and is in fact the divine spiritual person in its greatest form and image, heaven is therefore differentiated into members and parts like a person, and these are given similar names. Angels know what member one community or another is in and say that this community is in the member or province of the head, that one in the member of province of the chest, that one in the member or province of the genitals, and so on.[13]

The Kabbalists call this cosmic being Adam Kadmon, the androgynous primordial human. (*Adam* in Hebrew means "human being," not necessarily male.) The British Kabbalist Z'ev ben Shimon Halevi writes:

> Tradition . . . states that each person contains a spark of the original Adam deep within, and that the pursuit of completion arising from the sense of separation that everyone feels is the impulse of this spark seeking to return and become one with Adam Kadmon, who is the perfection of human possibility. We are in effect atoms of this great Image of God, and contain in miniature all the qualities and attributes of our ultimate ancestor and descendant, because at some point in the distant future, we shall be united as evolved atoms, to become cells of the organs and limbs of this Divine Being, who lives in that Eternal and unchanging realm of Light.[14]

Each of us, then, is a fragment of the cosmic Adam, who, in the world we know, experiences himself as a shattered being, his various cells and atoms divided and at odds with one another. The Great Work—which is the work of humanity as well as of each individual—is to restore this "Image of God" to its primordial harmony and unity. To do this, we must first accept *svadharma*, our own duty, which is to say our proper place and function in this cosmic being. This function is what each of us was created for; it was why we were brought into existence. It is the special role that each person has and only he or she can fill. In the language of Swedenborg or the Rig Veda, it may be in the "head"—that is, it may be of an intellectual type—or it may be in the "hands" or the "feet"—that is, of a more physical type. But to be in a different "member" or "part" is not to be inferior or superior, any more than a nerve cell is better or worse than a muscle cell.

A *Course in Miracles* is generally contemptuous of what it calls "specialness." Specialness is one of the chief ways in which the members of the separated Son of God (that is, Adam in his fallen state) reinforce their isolation. It is the ground of all separation and attack. "Specialness is the great dictator of the wrong decisions. Here is the grand illusion of what you are and what your brother is. . . . Specialness must be defended. He who is 'worse' than you must be attacked, so that your specialness can live on his defeat." The truth is the opposite. "Your brother is your friend because his Father created him like you. There is no difference. You have been given to each other that love might be extended, not cut off from one another. . . . Could you attack each other if you chose to see no specialness of any kind between you?"[15]

The *Course* makes one exception to its condemnation of specialness. This is the "special function." It is the means that the Holy Spirit—the force of atonement, in the *Course*'s theology—has chosen in order to transform specialness into a mode of healing:

> Such is the Holy Spirit's kind perception of specialness; His use of what you made, to heal instead of harm. To each He gives a special function in salvation he alone can fill; a part for only him. Nor is the plan complete until he finds his special function, and fulfills the part assigned to him, to make himself complete in a world where incompletion rules. . . .
>
> The Holy Spirit needs your special function, that His may be fulfilled. Think not you lack a special value here. You wanted it, and it is given you. . . .
>
> Your special function is the special form in which the fact that God is not insane appears most sensible and meaningful to you. The content is the same. The form is suited to your special needs, and to the special time and place in which you think you find yourself.[16]

The special function is each individual's *svadharma*. It is the specific role each of us has to play in the great plan of Atonement, in the restoration of the shattered Sonship to unity. As such, it goes far beyond caste or class or even career or profession as conventionally conceived.

For the Hindus, *svadharma* is intimately intertwined with *svabhava*, one's own being, the core of one's essence. To know your own work is to know your own being; you can't understand one without the other. For some people, the special function may involve wealth and position; for others, modest and humble circumstances. It may call one person onto the magnificent stage of history and may require another to spend his life in obscurity.

How do we find our special function? This is an extremely delicate issue, to be approached with great awareness and humility in oneself and even more when trying to see it in others. With the rarest exceptions, I don't believe it is possible to tell another person what his or her function is; it is a great enough thing to see one's own. People learn their special functions in many different ways and at many different times of life. One person knows hers from childhood; another discovers it only in middle age. It is revealed by still, small voices and by visions on the road to Damascus, but also sometimes in a career aptitude test or by answering an ad in the classifieds. It may remain steadfastly the same, a ridgepole on which one's entire life depends, or it may gradually change and shift forms as time and circumstances change. In any event, it has a single core feature: one has (or comes to have) the unshakable sense that this function, whatever it is, is why one exists, is what one was created to do.

Apart from this, it only seems possible to say what the special function is *not*. It is not necessarily something overtly "spiritual." The accountant who decides to chuck it all and become a massage therapist has not necessarily found her special function. She may be running away from her true responsibilities in a field where consciousness and integrity are very much needed. In certain cases an individual may even have to serve as the single spark of light and goodness in a corrupt organization. These situations are the most difficult and the most fraught with the risk of self-deception, since it is easy for someone to imagine he is serving the cause of integrity while steadily becoming corrupted himself.

Nor is the special function a type of spiritual busybodyness—running around and fixing what is wrong in everyone else, individually or collectively. Indeed, this is the fault of much activism. It seizes arbitrarily on one problem—abortion; global warming; the current war, whichever one it is; the current administration, whichever one it is—and this then becomes an *idée fixe*, an idol to which all else must be sacrificed. This kind of obsession can be found all along the ideological spectrum, although of course it's easier to see in one's opponents than in oneself. Gurdjieff remarks that the tendency "to grow indignant at the defects of others" makes modern human life, "already wretched and abnormal without this, objectively unbearable."[17]

There is a subtle but crucial difference between activism in this negative sense and working on current issues as part of one's special function (which may be necessary). The activist has an air of blind fanaticism about him; his eyes glaze over as he starts to rant about his favorite source of all evil. Another person, who may be working in ways that look almost identical from the exterior, does so consciously and with a sense of perspective. She is dedicated but not identified; she does the work with inner freedom and without attachment to results, as Krishna urges in the Gita. Moreover, the sense of scale is diametrically opposite in the two approaches. The activist bounces back and forth hysterically, deluging friends with frantic e-mails at the slightest sign of alarm; one who works from the special function tends to have more serenity and a greater sense of the long term. Some esotericists say that they are not working for today or tomorrow but for a century or two in the future.

The initial effect of finding, or at any rate glimpsing, one's special function is—ironically, it may seem, given all my remarks about the "I that is we"—to separate an individual from the herd. This tends to arouse contradictory emotions: a sense of superiority, perhaps, but also a feeling of isolation, of disillusionment with the things one used to take seriously. (In fact, the sense of superiority may be a kind of compensation for the isolation.) A man starts to feel colorless and unmotivated because his old motivations have begun to unravel. He finds that he has less in common with his family and friends than he once did. They may in turn carp at him for no longer being what he used to be. "And a man's foes shall be they of his own household" (Matthew 10:26). This can be heartbreaking. Very often it means that what one had taken to be love was so in only the most conditional and provisional sense. We usually don't see how many strings are attached to love until we break one or two of them.

For some people this isolation is long-standing. They work alone, guided only by their own inner truth. Most, however, soon gain companions on the path. After all, two men who are awake in a room with a hundred sleeping people will sooner or later find each other. They may be utterly dissimilar externally, in tastes or personality or social class, but the very fact that they are awake, at least to some degree, immediately gives them something profound in common. Frequently it means that they have a common task as well. They may look further and find others like them; they may also encounter someone who is slightly ahead of the rest in knowledge and ability and who becomes the leader. (As the familiar axiom has it, "When the student is ready, the master appears.") Thus is born what is sometimes called an esoteric "school" or "team."

For those who are just beginning, the primary purpose of this school seems to be their own individual development. Obviously, this is a necessary first step, but it is a first step only. Those who fail to realize this soon succumb to what Chögyam Trungpa called "spiritual materialism"—the obsession with "my" progress and "my" development. It is seeking enlightenment with one eye in the mirror. If either the group or the individuals in it are going to grow in any real sense, they will have to move past this elementary level and find their own task, the contribution they have to make to the life and spirit of their time—for esoteric schools and teams have their special functions as well.

Most of these teams have been extremely obscure; they have done their work in silence and have left at most a few faint traces in a text or monument. Others have been extremely visible. Such groups probably include the school that formed around Plato in the fourth century B.C., which took the knowledge of the old mystery schools and recast it into the language of the then-new discipline of philosophy; early Christianity, which provided a new religious vista for a world that had lost its faith in the pagan gods; the cathedral builders of early medieval France; the troubadours of medieval Provence, who made love the central focus of European culture; the Freemasons of the eighteenth century, who broke the back of political and religious tyranny in Western Europe; and the Theosophical Society of the late nineteenth century, which reintroduced the wisdom of the East to a Western world that was glutted with materialism. Not all such schools produce immediate results; in some cases their fruits appear long after the schools themselves, having completed their work, have vanished or ossified into empty shells.

This progression from personal development to what Gurdjieff's school calls "Work for the Work's sake" is, of course, a progression in maturity. It has nothing sentimental about it; it is quite matter-of-fact. A nine-year-old told to wash the dishes after dinner may whine, "Why? What's in it for me?" An adult who washes the dishes asks no such questions; the job has to be done because it is there.

It would be too glib, however, to say that this progression takes one from selfishness to selflessness. This is because selfishness and selflessness in a sense present a false dichotomy. There is an "either-or-ness" about them that is, given what we've seen already, essentially false. Work for the Work's sake is not for other people *apart from* oneself. It stems from the realization that the distinction between "other people" and oneself is ultimately illusory. Mahayana Buddhists speak of the *bodhisattva* vow, the vow that some practitioners take not to enter enlightenment themselves until all sentient beings are enlightened. On the surface this looks like a noble but somewhat crack-pated ideal; how long, after all, will it take for all beings to become enlightened? But the true insight of the teaching may be different. It suggests that enlightenment means recognizing that the individual mind that must be enlightened cannot be separated out from the collective mind. You can't put a pot of water on the stove and hope to boil the hydrogen atoms only.

The Buddhists speak of the liberation of all sentient beings; *A Course in Miracles* speaks of the Atonement; the Kabbalah speaks of the restoration of the cosmic Adam. All of these are nothing more than metaphors or manners of speaking. Even though they're superficially different, we can see their underlying similarity. They all portray life and existence as essentially a problem to be solved. This is natural, because humanity almost universally regards its existence as problematic. Man is the animal that believes something is wrong. Often we see the meaning and purpose of life as liberation from this "something wrong." But this attitude toward human destiny is itself only one of many that are possible. Some describe the project in more optimistic terms. Nicolas Berdyaev writes:

> Creative freedom gives rise to values. As a free being, a free spirit, man is called to be the creator of new values. The world of values is not a changeless ideal realm rising above man and freedom; it is constantly undergoing change and being created afresh. Man is free in relation to moral values, not merely in the sense that he is free to realize or not to realize them. . . . Man is free in the sense of being able to co-operate with God, to create the good and to produce new values. . . . Creative gifts and values are dynamic, and through them the creation of the world is going on.[18]

By this view, the place of humanity in the universe as we know it is not negative but positive. The world is not a nightmare from which we must awaken but rather an arena in which humans, individually and collectively and universally, can make manifest what Berdyaev calls "the source of creative energy which is realized in our life."[19] This, too, is a legitimate perspective; like the others, it casts its own unique light on the nature of reality and our place in it. The human enterprise will look one way viewed from a certain angle and another way viewed from a different one. Maybe it is by examining and absorbing as many of these perspectives as possible that we can best understand the special function that each of us, for reasons we can only dimly grasp, has been created to fulfill.

8

Transcending the Heart

It's difficult to write about love without feeling some obligation to launch into praises of the heart. The one has virtually become synonymous with the other. Mass culture has turned the ♥ symbol into an ideogram for love on Valentine's Day cards and T-shirts and bumper stickers. The heart is wiser than the head, we learn from many sources, particularly in New Age literature. Here is a fairly typical example, from the Life Positive Web site: "Head thinking is fractured and separatist, while heart thinking is holistic. . . . Head thinking . . . will look at one aspect of a situation at a time and draw conclusions based on that, while ignoring others. Modern civilization is a perfect example of head thinking, for all its systems are based on separatism. . . . Heart thinking is focused on reality and therefore unlikely to go too wrong."[1] Is this true?

One way to approach this question is by asking where we experience ourselves—that is, where in the body we feel the "I" is situated. Many people in modern civilization may feel as if the "I" is in the head somewhere a couple of inches behind the eyes. (This could help explain Descartes' famous claim that the connection between the body and the soul lies in the pineal gland, which sits roughly in that position.) People in other cultures may experience themselves quite differently. Carl Jung, during a visit to the southwestern United States, met a chief of the Taos Pueblo Indians named Ochwiay Biano. He relates part of a conversation they had:

> "See," Ochwiay Biano said, "how cruel the whites look. Their lips are thin, their noses sharp, their faces furrowed and distorted by folds. Their eyes have a staring expression; they are always seeking something. What are they seeking? The whites always want something; they are always uneasy and restless. We do not know what they want. We do not understand them. We think that they are mad."
>
> I asked him why he thought whites were all mad.
>
> "They say that they think with their heads," he replied.
>
> "Why of course. What do you think with?" I asked him in surprise.
>
> "We think here," he said, indicating his heart.[2]

Aristotle, who regarded the heart as the seat of all cognition (the brain being merely a mechanism for cooling the body)—would no doubt have sided with Ochwiay Biano, and indeed, in many languages the word for "heart" is intimately bound up not only with emotion and feeling but also with cognition. Some might also agree with Ochwiay Biano, and with the Life Positive article, that the mysterious process by which certain civilizations come to focus on the knowledge of the head is not progress but regression. Similar ideas are common in the world's mystical literature. The Persian poet Fakhr al-Din Iraqi writes:

> The first step in love
> is losing your head.
>
> After the petty ego,
> you then give up your life
> and bear the calamity.

With this behind you, proceed:
Polish the ego's rust
from the mirror of your self.[3]

Here the head, the rational mind, is portrayed as the seat of the ego. We must transcend it in order to reach the wisdom of the heart. "Your heart is the mirror / of the essence most high," writes another Persian poet, Shah Ni'matallah Wali.[4]

From all this it would be easy to conclude that the heart is always right and the head always wrong. As much as this thought might appeal to our sentimental side, it's probably too simplistic. For every song that praises the heart's wisdom, we might find another that laments its folly. It would also be mistaken to imagine that the world's mystics are unanimous about the superiority of the heart over the head. Sri Ram Chandra, a twentieth-century Indian spiritual master, observes, "Really speaking the heart is the gutter of humanity. We have to dive into this and do the work. Yes, once the *abhyasi* [spiritual practitioner] progresses and rises to the mind region, then the work becomes a pleasure. . . . In my own interest I move people quickly out of the heart region. After all, who would like to work there longer than necessary?"[5]

Ram Chandra's perspective is worth considering, since he was a master of a Hindu yogic tradition called Sahaj Marg ("natural way"). Sahaj Marg concentrates a great deal on the heart; indeed, its principal meditative practice is to focus on the light in the heart. But for a long time the emphasis is on cleaning this "gutter of humanity"—a procedure that, according to this tradition, requires esoteric practices performed by the master as well as the student.

For those reluctant to believe a Hindu yogi, the Bible may be more persuasive: "Who can say, I have made my heart clean, I am pure from sin?" (Proverbs 20:9). "He that trusteth in his own heart is a fool" (Proverbs 28:26). "The imagination of man's heart is evil from his youth" (Genesis 8:21). Verses such as these were used by the Kabbalists as evidence for their theory of *yetzer ha-ra*, the "evil impulse" that God has planted in the heart of man along with *yetzer ha-tov*, the "good impulse."

The heart and its impulses, then, are far more ambiguous in nature than some would admit. "He that trusteth in his own heart is a fool." How, then, can we say that all we need to do is follow the heart to find love? One may find love this way, but it probably won't be conscious love. It may prove to be willfully *unconscious* love.

Some of the answer lies in the purification of the heart, as the Sahaj Marg tradition suggests. If the heart is "the mirror of the essence most high," it is a mirror that needs to be carefully cleaned before it can reflect something more sublime than the defilements of day-to-day life. The process is a long and rigorous one, as we see in the allegorical cycles of the Grail quest. The knights ride out and endure many exploits in search of the Holy Grail, but only those with pure hearts find it. This may be because the Grail symbolizes the heart. According to the legend, it is the cup that Christ used at the Last Supper, when he transformed wine into blood, so the Grail is figuratively a cup that holds blood. Each of us also has a cup that holds blood: it is in the chest. Unless this cup is properly purified, it cannot receive the divine infusion that is represented by the vision of the Grail.[6]

For the knight in quest of the Grail, purity of heart may be enough. But there are those who may want more, who may sincerely wish for purity of heart but are reluctant to set the brain aside entirely. They may be more inspired by the exhortation in E. M. Forster's novel *Howards End*: "Only connect." It is connecting the head and the heart that Forster means.

What connects the head and the heart? Either one, working on its own, becomes what Christ in his parable characterizes as "an evil servant" who "shall begin to smite his fellowservants and to eat and drink with the drunken" (Matthew 24:48–50). Operating independently, both the heart and the head can become cruel and capricious masters. When the heart leads, the head has to run along behind, rationalizing the heart's irrational behavior. When the head leads, it usually turns into a cold and mechanical actuary. The parable asks, "Who then is a faithful and wise servant" who can manage the inner household of the individual soul while the master is away? Either the head or the heart, perhaps, provided that it is "faithful and wise," which does not happen extraordinarily often.

Christ goes on to speak of "the lord of that servant" who "will come in a day when he looketh not for him, and in an hour that he is not aware of." It is this "lord" that ultimately has to rule the "household" of the individual self. From what we have seen already, this "lord" cannot be either the head or the heart. Nor can it be the two taken together, since in the ordinary individual the two are not united; at best they enjoy an uneasy alliance, or rather truce.

A number of times in this book I have spoken of the true "I," that aspect of ourselves that *sees*, and does so from, as it were, a transcendental perspective; it can look on the operations of the entire self, the head and the heart and everything else, from a distance and thus clearly and compassionately. It is this "I" that is the "lord" of that "household." As the parable indicates, this lord is usually away. Buried in the subconscious mind, it exists but is scarcely operative. In the language of another parable, it is a "seed" that is sown in each of us but sometimes falls by the wayside, is sometimes eaten up by the birds of the air, and only occasionally matures to bear fruit (Matthew 13:3–11). In the language of still another parable, this "I" is the talents that the master gives to various of his servants. Some take the talents and multiply them with wise investments; one (the ordinary individual) simply takes his and buries it in the ground (Matthew 25:14–28). The "I" is given to all of us; we could not exist without it; but it is up to us whether we develop it (through spiritual practice, through rigorous inner examination, and through consciously enduring the mill of daily life) or simply bury it in a field of obliviousness.

To put a highly esoteric point in the plainest possible language, there is something in us that stands apart from the ceaseless flow of the head's thoughts and the equally ceaseless flow of the heart's feelings and can see them. It manifests in rare and unexpected moments of daily life. Many people who have had accidents say that as the accident was occurring, the nature of reality seemed to change for a few seconds. Time seemed to slow down, and there was a sense of watching the events from a remove, as if they were happening to someone else. Possibly this is an awakening of this "I" provoked by the shock of extreme surprise and danger. Those who want to have a connection with the "I" more regularly and in less traumatic circumstances often find that meditation of one sort or another provides such contact. The essence of meditation (at least in many of its forms) is a slow and painstaking detachment of the consciousness from its contents. An ancient Chinese text, the *Hui Ming Ching*, describes this process poetically:

> A radiance of Light surrounds the world of the mind.
> We forget each other, quiet and pure, all-powerful and
>   empty.
> Emptiness is lighted up by the radiance of the Heart of
>   Heaven.
> The sea is smooth and mirrors the moon on its surface.
> The clouds vanish in blue space,
> The mountains shine clear.
> Consciousness dissolves in vision.
> The disk of the moon floats solitary.[7]

"Consciousness dissolves in vision." The words sound paradoxical. How can one see when consciousness has dissolved? The line may be pointing to one of the results of this awakening. The mundane consciousness of the ego dissolves into a wider vision in which the "I" of the individual Self is no longer distinguished so rigidly from the "I that is we." The consciousness of the individual "I" becomes collective and in this way merges with the great Self of the cosmic human. That is why Christ can say, "I am the vine; ye are the branches" (John 15:5). Esoterically, "I am" is the vine to which all of us are joined as individual branches. To return to a previous metaphor, it is in this way that the seed of the "I" is planted in good ground. It grows to maturity and produces much fruit. Or like the mustard seed, it "becometh a tree, so that the birds of the air come and lodge in the branches thereof" (Matthew 13:32). It would be possible to go through practically all the parables of Christ, especially those that speak of the kingdom of heaven, and show how they cast light on the nature of this true "I." The same could be said of the Gospel of John, in which Christ does not speak in parables but in "I am" statements—"I am the vine"; "I am the door" (John 10:1); "I am the way, the truth, and the life" (John 14:6)—that convey other dimensions of the same message. Contrary to conventional Christianity, these statements refer not to the historical Jesus but to the Logos, the "I am" that is the true Self.

The metaphors for this paradoxical union, in which the Self is merged into a collective whole and yet retains and indeed realizes its identity, are numerous. We have seen a few in the course of this book. And yet metaphors are treacherous. They easily become gods in their own right. The best way to prevent this may not be to eradicate all metaphors but on the contrary to multiply them so that each one democratically does its part in conveying an aspect of truth and none can turn into a kind of Demiurge contending, "I am God, and no other."

With this in mind, I would like to add a metaphor of my own. Suppose that the universe consists of a limitless field of particles of light, infinitesimally small, smaller by far than even the most rarefied subatomic particles posited by current physics, and utterly indestructible. Each of these particles consists of nothing more than consciousness. And yet it is consciousness of a rather peculiar sort, one that enables each particle both to see and to be seen. Moreover, these particles are capable of joining with one another in an infinite number of combinations. As they *are seen*, these combinations form the objects that constitute reality at all levels; as they *see*, they form the individuals that behold them, each of which is imbedded with a degree of awareness that varies with its size and complexity. None of these combinations is permanent; they last for some duration and then dissolve, leaving the particles to recombine in other forms and other situations. But as these particles behold each other, their awareness is imbued with an appreciation that includes not only a recognition of the other but a joy and delight in its beauty. Like God himself, consciousness loves the world that it has made, and it becomes attached to what it experiences. It clings to the particularity of each combination, struggling to hold it together and in so doing making enemies of all the other forms that seem to challenge it. Out of this attachment arises all the sorrow of existence, because the nature of the universe is freedom and no form lasts or wishes to last forever. Thus comes not only dissolution but grief out of this dissolution; and thus love, as has long been known, is the root of all the joy in the universe and also of all its pain.

Notes

EPIGRAPH

This is an agraphon, or uncollected saying, of Jesus, found in Pseudo-Clement, *Homilies*, 2.51.1; 3.50.2; 18.20.4. Quoted in Schneemelcher, 1:91.

INTRODUCTION

1. Bukowski, 177.
2. Cicero, *De amicitia*, 81 [http://www.thelatinlibrary.com/cicero/amic.shtml], Feb. 2, 2007. My translation.
3. Quoted in Lilar, 143–44. Emphasis is in the original here and in other quotations unless otherwise noted.
4. See Longchenpa, 1:107.
5. Dante, *Paradiso*, 33.145; *Inferno*, 12:43. My translation.
6. For more on this distinction, see my *Inner Christianity*, 3.

CHAPTER ONE: KIERKEGAARD'S ERROR

1. Hohlenberg, 79–80.
2. Kierkegaard, *Letters and Documents*, xxv–xxvi.
3. Garff, 189. The censored word is as it appears in the source.
4. Kierkegaard, *Works of Love*, 25.

5. Plato, *Symposium*, 210a–211d. Plato's vision of erotic love in the *Symposium* is chiefly pedophilic, which is abhorrent to modern standards but in keeping with those of his day.

6. *Didache*, 1, in Staniforth, 191.

7. *The Shepherd of Hermas*, 29:1–2; in *The Apostolic Fathers*, 217.

8. Jerome, *Against Jovinianus*, 1.49 [http://www.people.fas.harvard.edu/~chaucer/canttales/wbpro/jer-men.html], Feb. 7, 2006. The first sentence is Jerome's quotation from an ancient authority named Xystus.

9. *Epistle of Barnabas*, 19; in Staniforth, 180. Emphasis added. For more on this point, see Nygren, 2:47–48.

10. Kierkegaard, *Works of Love*, 174–76. Emphasis is Kierkegaard's.

11. Kipnis, 93–94.

12. For more on Gurdjieff and his school, see Smoley and Kinney, ch. 9; see also my *Inner Christianity*, 40–42.

13. Gurdjieff, 361.

14. Berdyaev, 188.

15. Ibid.

16. Solovyov, 82.

17. Porphyry, *Life of Plotinus*, 2; quoted in the *Internet Encylopedia of Philosophy* [http://www.iep.utm.edu/n/neoplato.htm], Feb. 16, 2006.

18. François, duc de La Rochefoucauld, *Maxime* 330; my translation.

19. Liddell and Scott, s. v. *agapao*.

20. Yeats, "Vacillations," st. 4.

CHAPTER TWO: BEYOND THE EQUATION

1. Strauss, 439–48.

2. Ibid., 90.

3. Ibid., 37, 81.

4. Plato, *Lysis*, 206a, 210d.

5. Fein and Schneider, 1.

6. Strauss, 58.

7. Eduardo Porter and Michelle O'Donnell, "Facing Middle Age with No Degree and No Wife," *New York Times*, Aug. 5, 2006.

8. Fisher, 104.

9. Wilson, 43–44.

10. Ibid., 47.

11. Fromm, 3.

12. Gladwell, *Blink*.

13. Quoted in Ouspensky, 110.

14. Goleman, 291, 294–95.

15. The quotes, along with this outline of the process of falling in love, are found in Stendhal, 5–9.

16. Proust, 149–51.

17. Ibid., 171.

18. Ibid., 175.

19. Ibid., 292.

20. Nietzsche, *Beyond Good and Evil*, 84.

21. Jane Austen, *Emma*, ch. 8.

22. Leo Tolstoy, *Anna Karenina*, pt. 1, ch. 24.

23. Schopenhauer, 3:340. Emphasis in the original.

24. Fisher, 133–134.

25. Solovyov, 29.

26. Ibid., 51.

27. Ibid., 52.

28. Ibid., 54.

29. Nietzsche, *Thus Spoke Zarathustra*, 12.

30. Freud, *Civilization and Its Discontents*, 13.

31. The adage is often attributed to Aristotle, sometimes to Galen. Sometimes a rider is added: *praeter gallum mulieremque*, "except for the rooster and woman." For Aristotle's views on the connection between weakness and loss of semen, see *On the Generation of Animals*, 725b. See also Foucault, *The Use of Pleasure*, 133.

32. Lucretius, 4.1133–34. My translation.

33. For a comprehensive view of this process as it operates in philosophical schools, see Randall Collins's *Sociology of Philosophy*.

34. This was true at least for proto-Catholic Christianity, which later evolved into Catholicism and Orthodoxy. Other strains, such as certain Gnostic sects, maintained a more libertarian attitude.

35. Suetonius, *Tiberius*, para. 43; *Nero*, para. 28.

36. Juvenal, 6.116–30. My translation. Brittanicus was the son of Claudius by Messalina, later poisoned at the instigation of Claudius' stepson Nero.

37. On this point, see Fortune, 128.

38. Both Jerome and Cyprian are quoted in Hunt, 98–99.

39. Woods, 27–28.

40. Chang, 72–74; 103–07.

41. Ibid., 152–53.

42. Dante, *La Vita Nuova*, 31.

43. Hunt, 132–39.

44. Quoted in De Rougemont, 34.

45. Quoted in Markale, 209.

46. See De Rougemont, 83. For further discussion of the Cathars and their connection to courtly love, see my *Forbidden Faith*, 78–83.

47. Mouravieff, 2:235.

48. Ibid., 2:234, 240.

49. For more on this point, see Fortune, chs. 15–16.

50. Weininger, 29–31.

51. Mouravieff, 2:257.

52. I myself had some small involvement with this book, since it began as an article for *Gnosis*, a journal of the Western inner traditions of which I was then editor. See Cynthia Bourgeault, "Meeting in the Body of Hope," *Gnosis* 42 (Winter 1997), 46–53.

53. Bourgeault, *Love Is Stronger Than Death*, 26–27.

54. Ibid., 49, 89.

55. Ibid., 96.

56. Watters, 19.

57. For a recent discussion of polyamory, see Jorge N. Ferrer, "Monogamy, Polyamory, and Beyond," *Tikkun*, Jan.-Feb. 2007, 37ff.

58. On this point, see Gurdjieff, 806–10.

59. Quoted in Schuchard, 91.

60. Bourgeault, 44.

CHAPTER THREE: CONJUGIAL LOVE

1. Swedenborg used the Latin adjective *conjugialis* rather than the more customary *conjugalis*. Some scholars argue that he was attempting to make some distinction between the two, but this point is controversial. See Rose, Shotwell, and Bertucci, 289.

2. For a brief account of Swedenborg's life, see my essay "The Inner Journey of Emanuel Swedenborg" in Rose et al., 3–49.

3. Swedenborg, *Marital Love*, para. 459. Swedenborg numbered the paragraphs in his works, and because these are standard in all editions, I will use them for references to his writing.

4. Ibid., paras. 470, 476.

5. On this point, see Rose et al., 80.

6. This would seem to be contradicted by Luke 20:34–35: "The children of the world marry, and are given in marriage: but they which shall be accounted worthy to obtain that world, and the resurrection from the dead, neither marry, nor are given in marriage." Denying that this is literally the case in the heavenly realms, Swedenborg,

in *Marital Love*, para. 41, gives an allegorical interpretation of this verse, but it is not particularly convincing.

7. Swedenborg, *Marital Love*, para. 155.

8. Ibid., paras. 62, 65.

9. Ibid., para. 92.

10. Ibid., paras. 90–91, 100–01.

11. Barukh ben Abraham of Kosov, quoted in Matt, 157.

12. The Sanskrit word *tantra* comes from a root meaning "weaving." Some forms of Tantra, such as those found in Tibetan Buddhism, have no sexual component at all or may even involve intense asceticism. One common thread in many of these teachings is the use of things ordinarily regarded as forbidden—sex, wine, meat—as vehicles to enlightenment. The sense in which I am using it here is the one that has become most familiar in the West, whereby Tantra has come to be seen as a kind of sacralized sexuality. For discussions of these issues, see the introduction to Urban's *Tantra*; André Padoux, "What Do We Mean by Tantrism?" in Harper and Brown, 17–24; and Evola, 229.

13. Van Lysebeth, 272–73.

14. "Extremely Darwin: An Interview with Richard Dawkins," *California Wild*, 51 (Winter 1998) [http://www.calacademy.org/calwild/ 1998Winter/stories/darwin.html], Apr. 1, 2007. Bracketed material is in the interview.

15. Ibid.

16. My use of the term "real I" is similar but not identical to Mouravieff's as discussed in Chapter Two.

17. See Karen-Claire Voss, "The Hierosgamos Theme in the Images of the Rosarium Philosophorum" [www.istanbul-yes-istanbul.co.uk/ alchemy/Rosariumfinal.htm], July 31, 2006.

18. *A Course in Miracles*, Workbook, 419. *A Course in Miracles* is one of the greatest spiritual works of contemporary times. It was produced in the 1960s and 1970s by Helen Schucman, a New York psychologist who believed she was channeling (often quite unwillingly) the

voice of Jesus Christ. However one wishes to take this claim (and it would be impossible to verify one way or another), the *Course* remains one of the most profound expositions of esoteric Christianity ever to have been written. For more on the *Course*, see Smoley and Kinney, 63–66, and my *Inner Christianity*, 43–44.

19. John Wren-Lewis, "Gnosis: Goal or Ground?" *Gnosis* 34 (Winter 1995), 58.

20. Quoted in King, 55.

21. John Milton, *The Doctrine and Discipline of Divorce* [http://www. dartmouth.edu/ milton/reading_room/ddd/book_1], Aug. 4, 2006; preface and ch. 6.

22. Dan Hurley, "Divorce Rate: It's Not as High as You Think," *New York Times*, Apr. 19, 2005. See also "U.S. Divorce Statistics" [http: //www.divorcemag.com/statistics/statsUS.shtml]. The rates were approximately 25 percent in the postwar years and diminish as we go back in time. They were around 17 percent in 1930, 8 percent in 1910, and 5.5 percent in 1890 (Lewinsohn, 361).

23. Fortune, 5.

24. Wilson, 86.

25. Ovid, *Metamorphoses*, 8.708–10; my translation. Compare Needleman, 3–9.

26. Swedenborg, *Marital Love*, para. 47r.

CHAPTER FOUR: THE SELFISH SERPENT

1. Louisa May Alcott, *Little Women*, ch. 1.

2. Dawkins, 2.

3. Midgley, 144–45.

4. See the entry on Tomberg in Hanegraaff et al.

5. Tomberg, 142.

6. For further discussion of this subject, see my *Inner Christianity*, ch. 2.

7. Narby, 113.

8. Ibid., 117.

9. Ibid., 114–15.

10. N. O. Brown, 285.

11. Van Lysebeth, 274.

12. Merton, 119.

13. Dawkins, 206.

14. Joyce, 97–98.

15. *Tibetan Book of the Dead*, 289–90. The bracketed insertion is the translator's.

16. Freud, *Totem and Taboo*, 108.

17. Ibid., 122.

18. For the complete text of the *Enuma Elish*, see Bratcher; for further discussion, see Ricoeur, 175–83.

19. David Brown, "Genealogy Study Examines Price of Parenthood," *San Francisco Chronicle*, Jan. 16, 2007, A5.

20. Yeats, "Under Ben Bulben," 344.

21. Richard Smoley, "Heroic Virtue: An Interview with Brother David Steindl-Rast," *Gnosis* 24 (Summer 1992), 39.

CHAPTER FIVE: MAKING BROTHERS

1. Epicurus, *Vatican Aphorisms*, 52; quoted in Cyril Bailey, 1:65. My translation. For the following account of Epicurus and his philosophy, I am relying chiefly on Rist, especially ch. 7. See also de Botton, ch. 2.

2. Epicurus, *Fragments*, 39, quoted in de Botton, 56, 57.

3. Epstein, 243.

4. Burns, "Auld Lang Syne," in Quiller-Couch, 1:583.

5. World Burns Club, "Auld Lang Syne," 2004 [http://www. worldburnsclub.com/poems/translations/auld_lang_syne.htm], Aug. 14, 2007.

6. Bronislaw Malinowski, "The Primitive Economics of the Trobriand Islanders," *Economic Journal* (1921), 31:1–16 [http://melbecon. unimelb.edu.au/het/malinowski/prim], Dec. 24, 2006.

7. Quoted in Ouspensky, 151.

8. Nicoll, *Psychological Commentaries*, 1:254.

9. La Rochefoucauld, *Maximes*, 327, 441. My translations.

10. Quoted in Ouspensky, 153.

11. Shaw, "Maxims for Revolutionists," appendix to *Man and Superman*, in Shaw 3:731.

12. Qur'an 18:60–82.

13. Quoted in de Botton, 146.

14. Compare Aristotle, *Nicomachean Ethics*, 1169b7.

15. Quoted in de Botton, 147.

16. Florensky, 286.

17. Gustafson, "Introduction," in ibid., xx.

18. Epstein, 129. The quotation from Nietzsche is from *Human, All Too Human*.

19. Christopher Bamford, "The Joy of Two: Notes on Friendship in the Gospels," *Parabola* 29:4 (Winter 2004), 6.

20. Florensky, 327–28.

21. Ibid., 329.

22. Ibid., 287.

23. See my *Inner Christianity*, 226–27.

24. Nicoll, *New Man*, 79.

25. For more on the Gnostics, see my *Forbidden Faith*, especially ch. 1; see also Smoley and Kinney, ch. 2.

CHAPTER SIX: THE COSMIC HUMAN

1. "The Song of Prayer," 2.2.1–4 [http://www.unitedbeings.com/acim], Jan. 29, 2007.

2. Niebuhr, 2:56.

3. William Shakespeare, *Hamlet*, 2:2.

4. Cicero, *De amicitia*, 59. My translation.

5. My translation. Many English versions translate the second half of this verse as "as we forgive our debtors," but *aphekamen*, the verb here, is in the aorist tense, in this case more or less equivalent to the English perfect tense. See Smyth, 432–33.

6. At least in the English-speaking world. Jerome's Latin Vulgate, the official Bible of the Roman Catholic Church, has *debita*—again, "debts."

7. Brihadaranyaka Upanishad, 3.4.2; *The Thirteen Principal Upanishads*, 112.

8. Quoted in Alice Bailey, 38–39. Bailey is quoting an interview with Edison that appeared in *Harper's* in Feb. 1890.

9. Quoted in ibid., 41.

10. Schaya, 51.

11. That is, reason not in the conventional sense but in the sense of a higher, universal mind. See Martin Heidegger's essay "Logos," in Heidegger, ch. 2.

12. Gospel of Thomas, 77, in Robinson, 126.

13. Heraclitus, fragment 50 (DK); in Markovich, 115. The bracketed insertion is the translator's.

14. Heraclitus, fragment 2 (DK); in Markovich, 88. My translation.

15. Solovyov, *Lectures*, 123.

16. Coton-Alvart, 22. My translation; emphasis is Coton-Alvart's.

17. Corbin, 47, 48.

18. Irenaeus, "Against the Heretics," 1.18.1; quoted in Jonas, 42.

19. Mead, 262–63, 267. Mead is quoting the account of Basilides' teaching by the ancient heresiologist Hippolytus.

20. *A Course in Miracles*, Text, 519.

21. Kant, 111–12.

22. Ibid., 67.

23. Eliot, *The Waste Land*, sec. 5, in Eliot, 68.

24. Solovyov, *Lectures*, 164. Solovyov is quoting Romans 8:19, adding his own emphasis.

25. Zimmer, 285.

26. Rig Veda, 10.90; in O'Flaherty, 30–31.

27. *A Course in Miracles*, Workbook, 222.

28. Ibid., 242–43.

29. Trungpa, 11.

30. Acts of John, 11.20, in Robinson, 105.

31. Probably the most famous treatment of this theme is *Zanoni*, a nineteenth-century occult novel by Edward Bulwer Lytton, who was reputed to be an esoteric adept.

32. The word here translated as "life" is *psyche*, which, as noted earlier, is also often translated as "soul."

33. Pasternak, 43.

CHAPTER SEVEN: THE SPECIAL FUNCTION

1. Laxness, 408–09.

2. Wallis, 212–14.

3. Ezra Pound, "Ignite! Ignite!" in Smoley, *First Flowering*, 143. Spelling and punctuation are Pound's.

4. Schweitzer, 401.

5. R. E. Brown, 506.

6. Benedict XVI, *Deus caritas est*, Dec. 25, 2005, sec. 28a [http://www.vatican.va/holy_father/benedict_xvi/encyclicals/documents/hf_ben-xvi_enc_20051225_deus-caritas-est_en.html], Aug. 15, 2007.

7. Ibid., sec. 27.

8. Laqueur, 231–37. See my article "A Glimpse of Eastern Expanses," *Gnosis* 31 (Spring 1994), 10–13.

9. Gurdjieff, 636–37.

10. Bhagavad-Gita, 3.35, in Zaehner. Bracketed insertions are the translator's.

11. Ibid., 4.13.

12. Rig Veda, 10.90, in O'Flaherty, p. 31.

13. Swedenborg, *Heaven and Hell*, para. 65.

14. Halevi, 5.

15. *A Course in Miracles*, Text, 465, 466.

16. Ibid., 493, 495.

17. Gurdjieff, 1076–77.

18. Berdyaev, 44.

19. Ibid.

CHAPTER EIGHT: TRANSCENDING THE HEART

1. Suma Varughese, "Moving from Head to Heart," Life Positive, Sept. 2002 [http://www.lifepositive.com/Mind/personal-growth/personal-growth/heart-thinking.asp], Mar. 20, 2007.

2. Jung, 247–48.

3. Fideler and Fideler, 49.

4. Ibid., 23.

5. Quoted in Rajagopalachari, 90.

6. See my article "The Illumined Heart," *Gnosis* 51 (Spring 1999), 12–15.

7. Quoted in Wilhelm, 121.

Bibliography

Aland, Kurt, et al., eds. *The Greek New Testament*. 3rd ed. Reading, England: United Bible Societies, 1966.

Alighieri, Dante. *La Vita Nuova*. Barbara Reynolds, trans. Harmondsworth, England: Penguin, 1969.

The Apostolic Fathers. J. B. Lightfoot and J. R. Harmer, trans. 2nd ed. Grand Rapids, Mich.: Baker, 1989.

Aristotle. *The Basic Works of Aristotle*. Richard McKeon, ed. New York: Random House, 1941.

_____. *Ethica Nicomachea*. I. Bywater, ed. Oxford: Clarendon Press, 1890.

Bailey, Alice. *The Consciousness of the Atom*. New York: Lucis, 1922.

Bailey, Cyril, ed. *Lucretius: De rerum natura*. Text and commentary. 3 vols. Oxford: Clarendon Press, 1947.

Balzac, Honoré de. *The Physiology of Marriage*. Sharon Marcus, ed. Baltimore: Johns Hopkins University Press, 1997.

Bataille, Georges. *Erotism, Death, and Sensuality*. Mary Dalwood, trans. San Francisco: City Lights Books, 1986.

Berdyaev, Nicolas. *The Destiny of Man*. Natalie Duddington, trans. New York: HarperCollins, 1960.

Besant, Annie. *Esoteric Christianity*. Richard Smoley, ed. Wheaton, Ill.: Quest, 2006.

Bourgeault, Cynthia. *Love Is Stronger Than Death*. 2nd ed. Great Barrington, Mass.: Lindisfarne, 2001.

Bratcher, Richard. "Enuma Elish: 'When on High . . .': The Mesopotamian/ Babylonian Creation Myth," 2006 [http://www.crivoice.org/enumaelish .html], Aug. 14, 2007.

Brown, Norman O. *Life Against Death: The Psychoanalytical Meaning of History.* Middletown, Conn.: Wesleyan University Press, 1959.

Brown, Raymond E. *Introduction to the New Testament.* New York: Doubleday, 1997.

Bukowski, Charles. *Notes of a Dirty Old Man.* San Francisco: City Lights Books, 1973.

Chang, Stephen T. *The Tao of Sexology: The Book of Infinite Wisdom.* San Francisco: Tao, 1986.

Collins, Randall. *The Sociology of Philosophy: A Global Theory of Intellectual Change.* Cambridge, Mass.: Harvard University Press, 1998.

The Complete Kama Sutra. Alain Daniélou, trans. Rochester, Vt.: Park Street Press, 1994.

Corbin, Henry. *Spiritual Body and Celestial Earth from Mazdean Iran to Shi'ite Iran.* Nancy Pearson, trans. Princeton, N.J.: Princeton/Bollingen, 1977.

Coton-Alvart, Henri. *Les deux lumières: La science de la nature vivante dans ses mutations.* Paris: Dervy, 1996.

A Course in Miracles. 3 vols. Tiburon, Calif.: Foundation for Inner Peace, 1975.

Dawkins, Richard. *The Selfish Gene.* New York: Oxford University Press, 1976.

de Botton, Alain. *The Consolations of Philosophy.* New York: Vintage, 2001.

De Rougemont, Denis. *Love in the Western World.* Montgomery Belgion, trans. Rev. ed. Princeton, N.J.: Princeton University Press, 1983.

Eliot, T. S. *Collected Poems, 1909–62.* New York: Harcourt, 1963.

Epstein, Joseph. *Friendship: An Exposé.* Boston: Houghton Mifflin, 2007.

Evola, Julius. *The Metaphysics of Sex.* Deborah Forman, trans. New York: Inner Traditions, 1983.

Fein, Ellen, and Sherrie Schneider. *The Rules: Time-Tested Secrets for Capturing the Heart of Mr. Right.* New York: Warner Books, 1995.

Fideler, David, and Sabrineh Fideler, trans. *Love's Alchemy: Poems from the Sufi Tradition.* Novato, Calif.: New World Library, 2006.

Fisher, Helen. *Why We Love: The Nature and Chemistry of Romantic Love.* New York: Henry Holt, 2004.

Florensky, Pavel. *The Pillar and Ground of Truth: An Essay in Orthodox Theodicy in Twelve Letters.* Boris Jakim, trans. Princeton, N.J.: Princeton University Press, 1997.

Fortune, Dion. *The Esoteric Philosophy of Love and Marriage.* London: Aquarian Press, 1967. Originally published 1924.

Foucault, Michel. *The History of Sexuality*, Vol. 1: *An Introduction.* Robert Hurley, trans. New York: Pantheon, 1978.

_____. *The History of Sexuality*, Vol. 2: *The Use of Pleasure*. Robert Hurley, trans. New York: Vintage, 1990.

Freud, Sigmund. *Civilization and Its Discontents*. James Strachey, trans. New York: Norton, 1961.

_____. *Totem and Taboo: Resemblances Between the Psychic Lives of Savages and Neurotics*. A. A. Brill, trans. Minneola, N.Y.: Dover, 1998.

Fromm, Erich. *The Art of Loving*. New York: Harper Perennial, 1989. Originally published 1956.

Garff, Joakim. *Søren Kierkegaard: A Biography*. Bruce H. Kirmmse, trans. Princeton, N.J.: Princeton University Press, 2005.

Garrison, Omar. *Tantra: The Yoga of Sex*. New York: Julian Press, 1964.

Gladwell, Malcolm. *Blink: The Power of Thinking Without Thinking*. New York: Little, Brown, 2005.

Goleman, Daniel. *Emotional Intelligence*. New York: Bantam, 1995.

Gracian, Baltasar. *A Truthtelling Manual and the Art of Worldly Wisdom*. Martin Fischer, trans. Rev. ed. Springfield, Ill.: Thomas, 1945.

Gray, John. *Men Are from Mars, Women Are from Venus*. New York: Harper-Collins, 1992.

Gurdjieff, G. I. *All and Everything: Beelzebub's Tales to His Grandson*. New York: Dutton, 1950.

Halevi, Z'ev ben Shimon. *The Work of the Kabbalist*. York Beach, Maine: Weiser, 1986.

Handelman, Don, and David Shulman. *God Inside Out: Siva's Game of Dice*. New York: Oxford University Press, 1997.

Hanegraaff, Wouter J., et al., eds. *Dictionary of Gnosis and Western Esotericism*. 2 vols. Leiden, Netherlands: Brill, 2005.

Harper, Katherine Anne, and Robert L. Brown, eds. *The Roots of Tantra*. Albany: State University of New York Press, 2002.

Heidegger, Martin. *Early Greek Thinking*. David Farrell Krell and Frank A. Capuzzi, trans. New York: HarperCollins, 1975.

Hoffman, Bob. *No One Is to Blame: Getting a Loving Divorce from Mom and Dad*. Palo Alto, Calif.: Science and Behavior Books, 1979.

Hohlenberg, Johannes. *Sören Kierkegaard*. T. H. Croxall, trans. New York: Pantheon, 1954.

The Holy Qur'an: Arabic Text, English Translation, and Commentary. Maulana Muhammad Ali, trans. 6th ed. Chicago: Specialty Publications, 1973.

Hunt, Morton M. *The Natural History of Love*. New York: Knopf, 1959.

Jonas, Hans. *The Gnostic Religion*. 2nd ed. Boston: Beacon Press, 1963.

Joyce, James. *Dubliners: Text, Criticism, and Notes*. Robert Scholes and
    A. Walton Litz, eds. New York: Viking, 1969.

Jung, Carl G. *Memories, Dreams, Reflections*. Richard Winston and Clara
    Winston, eds. Rev. ed. New York: Vintage, 1973.

Kant, Immanuel. *Prolegomena to Any Future Metaphysics*. Lewis White Beck, ed.
    Indianapolis: Bobbs-Merrill, 1950.

Kierkegaard, Søren. *Letters and Documents*. Henrik Rosenmeier, trans. Princeton,
    N.J.: Princeton University Press, 1978.

———. *Works of Love*. Howard Hong and Edna Hong, trans. New York: Harper-
    Collins, 1962.

King, Francis. *Tantra for Westerners: A Practical Guide to the Way of Action*. New
    York: Destiny, 1986.

Kipnis, Laura. *Against Love*. New York: Vintage, 2003.

Laqueur, Walter. *Black Hundred: The Rise of the Extreme Right in Russia*. New
    York: HarperCollins, 1993.

La Rochefoucauld, François de. *Réflexions ou sentences et maximes morales*. Paris:
    Garnier, 1961.

Laurence, Tim. *The Hoffman Process*. New York: Bantam, 2003.

Laxness, Halldór. *World Light*. Magnus Magnusson, trans. New York: Vintage,
    2002.

Legman, Gershom. *No Laughing Matter: Rationale of the Dirty Joke, Second Series*.
    New York: Breaking Point, 1975.

———. *Oragenitalism*. New York: Julian Press, 1969.

———. *Rationale of the Dirty Joke: An Analysis of Sexual Humor*. New York:
    Castle, 1968.

Lewinsohn, Richard. *A History of Sexual Customs*. Alexander Mace, trans. New
    York: Premier, 1962.

Lewis, Thomas, Fari Amini, and Richard Lannon. *A General Theory of Love*. New
    York: Vintage, 2001.

Liddell, Henry George, and Robert Scott. *A Greek-English Lexicon*. Henry Stuart
    Jones, ed. Oxford: Clarendon Press, 1968.

Lilar, Suzanne. *Aspects of Love in Western Society*. Jonathan Griffin, trans. New
    York: McGraw-Hill, 1965.

Longchenpa. *Kindly Bent to Ease Us: The Trilogy of Finding Comfort and Ease*.
    Herbert V. Guenther, trans. and ed. 3 vols. Berkeley, Calif.: Dharma Pub-
    lishing, 1975–76.

Marion, Jean-Luc. *The Erotic Phenomenon*. Stephen E. Lewis, trans. Chicago:
    University of Chicago Press, 2007.

Markale, Jean. *Courtly Love: The Path of Sexual Initiation.* Jon Graham, trans. Rochester, Vt.: Inner Traditions, 2000.

Markovich, M., ed. *Heraclitus: Greek Text with a Short Commentary.* Merida, Venezuela: Los Andes University Press, 1967.

Matt, Daniel C., ed. *The Essential Kabbalah.* San Francisco: HarperSanFrancisco, 1995.

Mead, G.R.S. *Fragments of a Faith Forgotten: The Gnostics; a Contribution to the Study of Early Christianity.* New Hyde Park, N.Y.: University Books, 1960. Originally published 1900.

Melina, Livio, and Carl A. Anderson, eds. *The Way of Love: Reflections on Pope Benedict XVI's Encyclical* Deus caritas est. San Francisco: Ignatius, 2006.

Merton, Thomas. *The New Man.* New York: Farrar, Straus, and Cudahy, 1961.

Midgley, Mary. *Evolution as a Religion.* Rev. ed. London: Routledge, 2002.

Milton, John. *The Complete Poems of John Milton.* New York: Crown, 1936.

Mouravieff, Boris. *Gnôsis: Étude et commentaire sur la tradition ésotérique de l'orthodoxie orientale.* 3 vols. Neuchâtel, Switzerland: À la Baconnière, 1969–72.

———. *Gnosis: Study and Commentaries on the Esoteric Tradition of Eastern Orthodoxy.* S. A. Wissa, Maneck d'Oncieu, and Robin Amis, trans. 3 vols. Newburyport, Mass.: Praxis Institute Press, 1989–93.

Narby, Jeremy. *The Cosmic Serpent: DNA and the Origins of Knowledge.* New York: Tarcher/Putnam, 1998.

Nicoll, Maurice. *The New Man: An Interpretation of Some Parables and Miracles of Christ.* Boulder, Colo.: Shambhala, 1984.

———. *Psychological Commentaries on the Teaching of Gurdjieff and Ouspensky.* 5 vols. York Beach, Maine: Weiser, 1996.

Niebuhr, Reinhold. *The Nature and Destiny of Man: A Christian Interpretation.* 2 vols. Louisville, Ky.: Westminster/John Knox, 1996.

Nietzsche, Friedrich. *Beyond Good and Evil: Prelude to a Philosophy of the Future.* Walter Kaufmann, trans. New York: Viking, 1966.

———. *Thus Spoke Zarathustra.* Walter Kaufmann, trans. New York: Viking, 1966.

Nygren, Anders. *Agape and Eros.* Philip Watson, trans. 3 vols. London: SPCK, 1938.

O'Flaherty, Wendy Doniger, ed. and trans. *The Rig Veda.* Harmondsworth, England: Penguin, 1981.

The Ordinances of Manu. Arthur Coke Burnell, trans. New Delhi: Munshiram Manoharlal, 1995. Originally published 1884.

Otto, Rudolf. *The Idea of the Holy.* John W. Harvey, trans. Rev. ed. London: Oxford University Press, 1928.

Ouspensky, P. D. *In Search of the Miraculous: Fragments of a Forgotten Teaching.* New York: Harcourt, 1949.

Ovid. *The Art of Love and Other Poems.* J. H. Mozley and G. P. Gould, trans. Cambridge, Mass.: Loeb Classical Library, 1979.

———. *Metamorphoseon libri 1–15.* B. A. van Proosdij, ed. Leiden, Netherlands: Brill, 1975.

Pasternak, Boris. *Doctor Zhivago.* Max Hayward and Manya Harari, trans. New York: Pantheon, 1958.

Persius and Juvenal. *Saturae.* W. V. Clausen, ed. Oxford: Clarendon Press, 1959.

Plato. *The Collected Dialogues.* Edith Hamilton and Huntington Cairns, eds. Princeton, N.J.: Princeton/Bollingen, 1961.

Proust, Marcel. *Swann's Way.* C. K. Scott Moncrieff, trans. New York: Vintage, 1970.

Quiller-Couch, Arthur, ed. *The Oxford Book of English Verse.* 2 vols. Rev. ed. Oxford: Clarendon Press, 1939.

Rajagopalachari, Parthasarathi. *My Master: The Essence of Pure Love.* Molena, Ga.: Sri Ram Chandra Mission, 1975.

Ricoeur, Paul. *The Symbolism of Evil.* Emerson Buchanan, trans. New York: HarperCollins, 1967.

Rist, J. M. *Epicurus: An Introduction.* Cambridge: Cambridge University Press, 1972.

Robinson, James M., ed. *The Nag Hammadi Library in English.* San Francisco: HarperSanFrancisco, 1977.

Rose, Jonathan, Stuart Shotwell, and Mary Lou Bertucci, eds. *Emanuel Swedenborg: Essays for the New Century Edition on His Life, Work, and Impact.* West Chester, Pa.: Swedenborg Foundation, 2005.

Schaya, Leo. *The Universal Meaning of the Kabbalah.* Nancy Pearson, trans. London: Unwin, 1971.

Schneemelcher, Wilhelm, ed. *New Testament Apocrypha.* 2 vols. R. M. Wilson et al., trans. Cambridge: Clarke, 1991.

Schopenhauer, Arthur. *The World as Will and Idea.* R. B. Haldane and J. Kemp, trans. 3 vols. London: Routledge, 1883.

Schuchard, Marsha Keith. *Why Mrs. Blake Cried: William Blake and the Sexual Basis of Spiritual Vision.* London: Century, 2006.

Schweitzer, Albert. *The Quest of the Historical Jesus: A Study of Its Progress from Reimarus to Wrede.* W. Montgomery, trans. New York: Macmillan, 1961.

Shaw, George Bernard. *Complete Plays with Prefaces.* 6 vols. New York: Dodd, Mead, 1963.

Sigstedt, Cyriel Odhner. *The Swedenborg Epic: The Life and Works of Emanuel Swedenborg.* London: Swedenborg Society, 1981.

Smoley, Richard. *Forbidden Faith: The Gnostic Legacy from the Gospels to* The Da Vinci Code. San Francisco: HarperSanFrancisco, 2006.

———. *Inner Christianity: A Guide to the Esoteric Tradition.* Boston: Shambhala, 2002.

Smoley, Richard, ed. *First Flowering: The Best of the Harvard Advocate, 1876–1976.* Reading, Mass.: Addison-Wesley, 1977.

Smoley, Richard, and Jay Kinney. *Hidden Wisdom: A Guide to the Western Inner Traditions.* Rev. ed. Wheaton, Ill.: Quest, 2006.

Smyth, Herbert Weir. *Greek Grammar.* Cambridge, Mass.: Harvard University Press, 1920.

Solovyov, Vladimir. *Lectures on Divine Humanity.* Peter Zouboff, trans. Hudson, N.Y.: Lindisfarne. 1995.

———. *The Meaning of Love.* Thomas R. Beyer Jr. and Jane Marshall, trans. Hudson, N.Y.: Lindisfarne, 1995.

Spiegelberg, Friedrich. *The Religion of Non-Religion.* London: Buddhist Lodge, 1938.

Staniforth, Maxwell, ed. and trans. *Early Christian Writings.* Harmondsworth, England: Penguin, 1968.

Stendhal. *On Love.* "H.B.V." and C. K. Scott Moncrieff, trans. New York: Liveright, 1927.

Stopes, Marie. *Married Love.* Ross McKibbin, ed. Oxford: Oxford University Press, 2004.

Strauss, Neil. *The Game: Penetrating the Secret Society of Pickup Artists.* New York: HarperCollins, 2005.

Swedenborg, Emanuel. *Heaven and Hell.* George F. Dole, trans. Rev. ed. West Chester, Pa.: Swedenborg Foundation, 2000.

———. *Marital Love: Its Wise Delights.* William Frederic Wunsch, trans. New York: Swedenborg Foundation, 1973.

———. *True Christianity*, vol. 1. Jonathan S. Rose, trans. West Chester, Pa.: Swedenborg Foundation, 2006.

The Thirteen Principal Upanishads. R. E. Hume, trans. Rev. ed. London: Oxford University Press, 1931.

The Tibetan Book of the Dead. Gyurme Dorje, trans. New York: Viking, 2005.

Tolstoy, Lev. *Anna Karenina.* Margaret Wettlin, trans. 2 vols. Moscow: Progress Publishers, 1978.

Tomberg, Valentin. *Meditations on the Tarot: A Journey into Christian Hermeticism*. Robert A. Powell, trans. Warwick, N.Y.: Amity House, 1985.

Trungpa, Chögyam. *Glimpses of Abhidharma*. Boston: Shambhala, 2001.

Urban, Hugh B. *Tantra: Sex, Secrecy, Politics, and Power in the Study of Religion*. Berkeley: University of California Press, 2003.

Van Lysebeth, André. *Tantra: The Cult of the Feminine*. York Beach, Maine: Weiser, 1995.

Wallis, Jim. *God's Politics: Why the Right Gets It Wrong and the Left Doesn't Get It*. San Francisco: HarperSanFrancisco, 2005.

Watters, Ethan. *Urban Tribes: Are Friends the New Family?* New York: Bloomsbury, 2003.

Watts, Alan. *In My Own Way*. New York: Pantheon, 1972.

Weininger, Otto. *Sex and Character*. London: Heinemann, 1906.

Wilhelm, Richard, trans. *The Secret of the Golden Flower: A Chinese Book of Life*. With commentary by C. G. Jung. New York: Causeway, 1975. Originally published 1931.

Wilson, James Q. *The Marriage Problem: How Our Culture Has Weakened Families*. New York: HarperCollins, 2002.

Woods, Margo. *Masturbation, Tantra, and Self-Love*. San Diego, Calif.: Omphaloskepsis Press, 1981.

Yeats, William Butler. *The Collected Poems of W. B. Yeats*. Rev. ed. New York: Macmillan, 1956.

Zaehner, R. C., ed. and trans. *The Bhagavad-Gita*. London: Oxford University Press, 1969.

Zimmer, Heinrich. *Philosophies of India*. Joseph Campbell, ed. London: Routledge & Kegan Paul, 1951.

About the Author

Richard Smoley has over thirty years' experience in studying and practicing the Western esoteric traditions. Educated at Harvard and Oxford Universities, he is the author of *Inner Christianity: A Guide to the Esoteric Tradition*; *Forbidden Faith: A Secret History of Gnosticism*; *The Essential Nostradamus*; and (with Jay Kinney) *Hidden Wisdom: A Guide to the Western Inner Traditions*. Formerly editor of *Gnosis* magazine, he is now editor of Quest Books. He currently lives in western Massachusetts.

Index